fashion
details

fashion details

1,000 IDEAS FROM NECKLINE TO WAISTLINE, POCKETS TO PLEATS

BEVERLY MASSACHUSETTS

ROCKPORT PUBLISHERS

Copyright © 2011 by **maomao** publications
First published in 2011 in the United States of America by
Rockport Publishers, a member of Quayside Publishing Group
100 Cummings Center
Suite 406-L
Beverly, MA 01915-6101
Telephone: (978) 282-9590
Fax: (978) 283-2742
www.rockpub.com

ISBN-13: 978-1-59253-716-7
ISBN-10: 1-59253-716-2

10 9 8 7 6 5 4 3 2 1

Publisher: Paco Asensio
Editorial coordination: Anja Llorella Oriol
Text edition: Natalio Martín Arroyo
Art director: Emma Termes Parera
Layout: Esperanza Escudero Pino
English translation: Cillero & de Motta

Editorial Project:
maomao publications
Via Laietana, 32 4th fl. of. 104
08003 Barcelona, España
Tel. : +34 93 268 80 88
Fax : +34 93 317 42 08
www.maomaopublications.com

Printed in Singapore

contents

A small detail makes a big difference

The saying that small details make a big difference is certainly not new. We are all aware of the significance. In fact, in any differential marketing strategy, a product is special and different from the rest for those details that make it unique. In fashion, the same rules apply. Proof of this are those details that are now trademarks for many fashion houses such as the Chanel neckline by the French designer, which Karl Lagerfeld has reinvented year after year, and the flounces patented by the prestigious Spanish designers Victorio & Lucchino that they call "caracola." There are also those details that have become icons of an era, such as the Gaultier's cone-shaped corset created for Madonna's Blond Ambition Tour, which was an emblematic symbol of fashion in the early nineties.

The history of costume shows us the important role that details have played in fashion over the years. For centuries, they have defined the distinctive features of each period and the differentiation between social classes and groups. Each moment has contributed new elements that represent an infinite source of inspiration for designers all over the world. The magic of fashion is its consistent ability to evolve, combining new materials with more traditional materials, inventing and reviving past fashions. It is not an easy task to reinterpret elements from other times and cultures, however, with careful research, many designers have been captivated by past practices and have managed to reinterpret them. Details from former times are constantly reappearing on international runways such as the Baroque Medici collar

and the Renaissance ruffled sleeves. Other details come from far-off places, made with techniques such as Japanese origami or embroidery with designation of origin, such as traditional Paraguayan Ñandutí lace or French knots.

In this book we visit fashion weeks in New York, Paris, Milan, London, Madrid, Copenhagen, Berlin, Mexico, Lisbon, Moscow, Tokyo, and many more, with collections featuring both classic and more revolutionary styles, through which we will show international trends and the most eye-catching details in current fashion. Designers such as Manish Arora, Maison Martin Margiela, Tsumori Chisato, and Kris Van Assche are featured along with some of the major names in fashion. In addition, new hopes from first class design schools bring an air of freshness to the amazing talent featured in this project. In these times of imminent globalization, the fashion industry researches and becomes immersed in the pursuit for ethnic and cultural values salvaged from remote civilizations. For this reason, we have included a selection of designers from over twenty different countries whose designs and the care with which the details are made are an example of the cultural richness that we have yet to discover and the contribution that intercultural exchange can offer a market such as the fashion industry.

Experience *Fashion Details*—a universe of details categorized into eight chapters that invite you to take a fresh look at the world of fashion and all of its endless possibilities.

COLLARS AND NECKLINES

A garment's neckline or collar is often the secret weapon to turn a simple garment into a sublime garment, which also gives the wearer one personality or another: casual, sensual, romantic, or elegant. Many of them are revived and changed according to the era. A perfect example is the halterneck, which was a runaway success for evening gowns in the thirties; then it became popular in the seventies by labels such as Halston, and at the start of this century it regained strength again. This chapter offers an extensive selection of collars and necklines used in the latest international collections. We will take a look at well-defined models, which in themselves are the key to the whole outfit, and others that are complemented with appliqués and accessories that make the outfit stand out. They are all here, from the classic round necks, V-necks, crew necks, and turtlenecks, to boat necks, mao necks, asymmetrical, strapless, etc. Explore endless interpretations of necklines and elaborate designs that convert collars into works of art, architectural pieces, or divine jewels.

001 AMERICAN PÉREZ
SPAIN

002 THE SWEDISH SCHOOL
OF TEXTILES
SWEDEN

003 ANJARA
SPAIN

© Kristian Löveborg

004 ANJARA
SPAIN

005 THE SWEDISH SCHOOL
OF TEXTILES
SWEDEN

006 AMERICAN PÉREZ
SPAIN

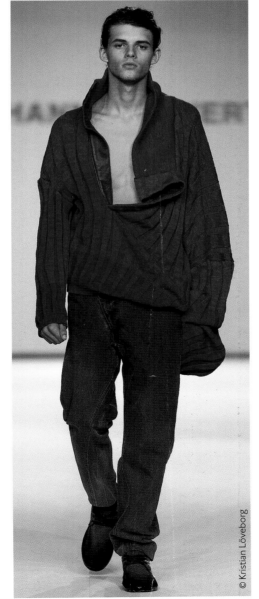

© Kristian Löveborg

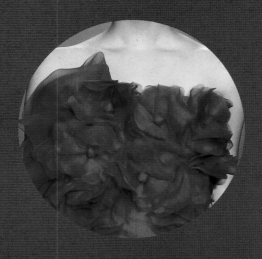

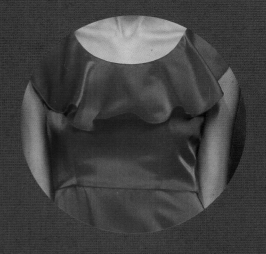

007 ELISA PALOMINO
SPAIN

008 TSUMORI CHISATO
JAPAN

009 BEBA'S CLOSET
SPAIN

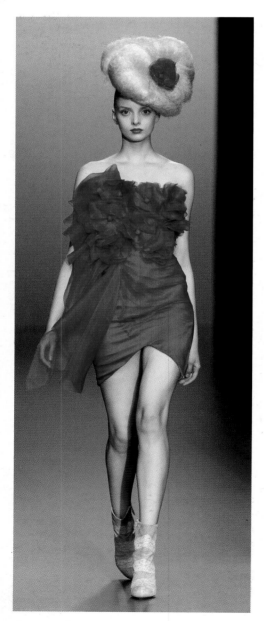

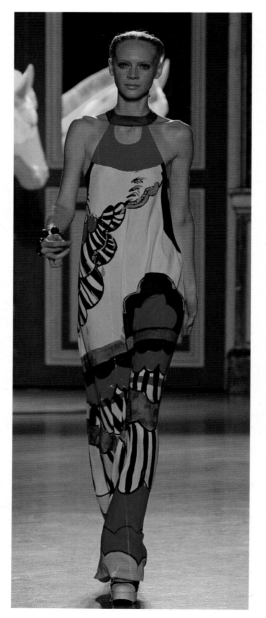

010 MANISH ARORA
INDIA

011 BORA AKSU
TURKEY

012 VICTORIO & LUCCHINO
SPAIN

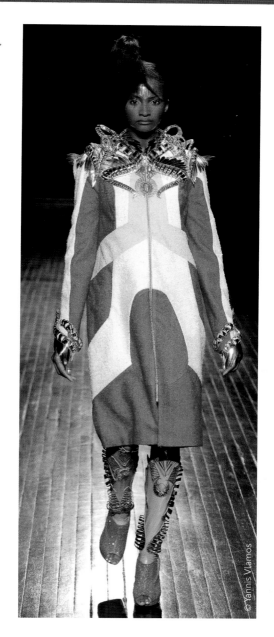

013 ANA LOCKING
SPAIN

014 MANISH ARORA
INDIA

015 TSUMORI CHISATO
JAPAN

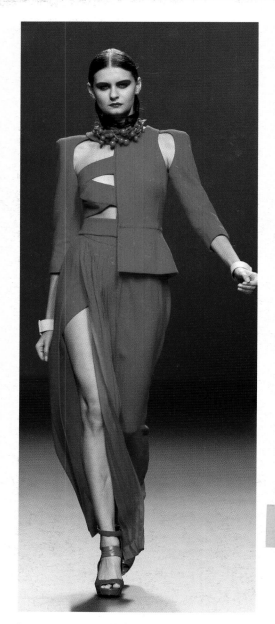

016 DIMITRI
ITALY

017 MANISH ARORA
INDIA

018 ANA LOCKING
SPAIN

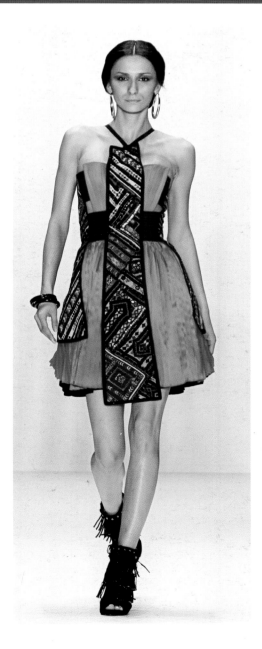

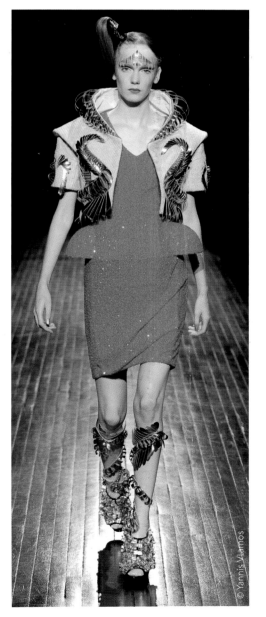

019 THE SWEDISH SCHOOL
OF TEXTILES
SWEDEN

020 LEMONIEZ
SPAIN

021 CATI SERRÀ
SPAIN

© Kristian Löveborg

022 MARTA MONTOTO
SPAIN

023 CATI SERRÀ
SPAIN

024 MALINI RAMANI
USA/INDIA

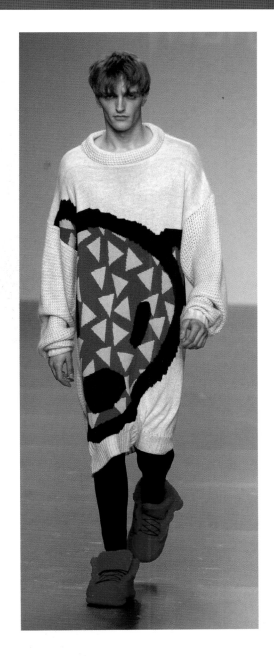

025 BIBIAN BLUE
SPAIN

026 THE SWEDISH SCHOOL
OF TEXTILES
SWEDEN

027 DIMITRI
ITALY

© Kristian Löveborg

028 BOHENTO
SPAIN

029 MALINI RAMANI
USA/INDIA

030 ALI CHARISMA
INDONESIA

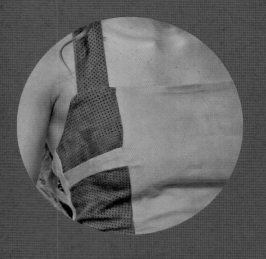

031 BOHENTO
SPAIN

032 MARTA MONTOTO
SPAIN

033 THE SWEDISH SCHOOL
OF TEXTILES
SWEDEN

© Kristian Löveborg

034 MARTIN LAMOTHE
SPAIN

035 CHARLIE LE MINDU
FRANCE

036 AILANTO
SPAIN

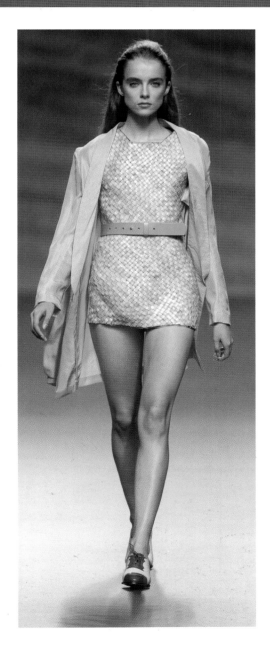

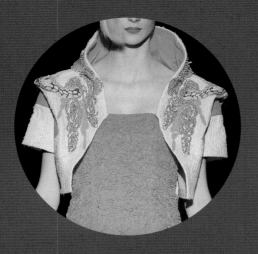

037 MANISH ARORA
INDIA

038 EK THONGPRASERT
THAILAND

039 MANISH ARORA
INDIA

©Yannis Vlamos

©Yannis Vlamos

040 BOHENTO
SPAIN

041 MAL-AIMÉE
FRANCE

042 ERICA ZAIONTS
UKRAINE

043 G.V.G.V.
JAPAN

044 THE SWEDISH SCHOOL
OF TEXTILES
SWEDEN

045 JUANJO OLIVA
SPAIN

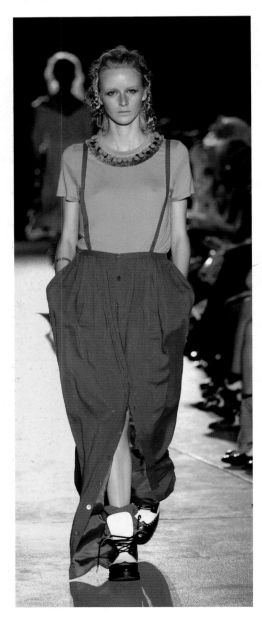

© Kristian Löveborg

046 THE SWEDISH SCHOOL
OF TEXTILES
SWEDEN

047 MALAFACHA BRAND
MEXICO

048 THE SWEDISH SCHOOL
OF TEXTILES
SWEDEN

© Kristian Löveborg

© Israel Esparza

© Kristian Löveborg

049 ALENA AKHMADULLINA
RUSSIA

050 DIANA DORADO
COLOMBIA

051 QASIMI
UNITED ARAB EMIRATES

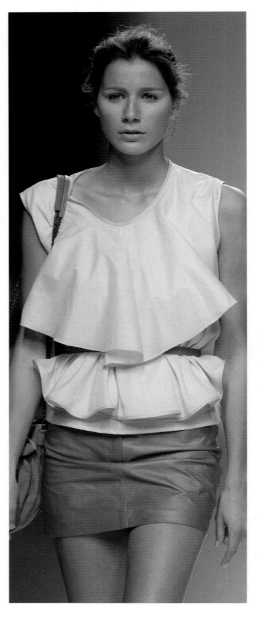

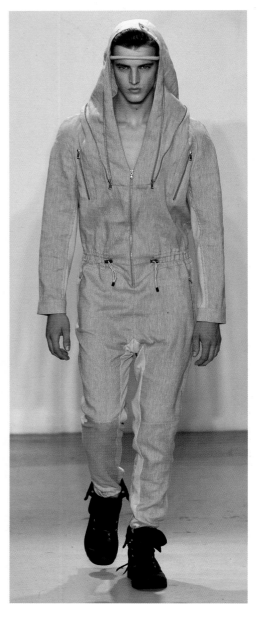

052 DIANA DORADO
COLOMBIA

053 IDA SJÖSTEDT
SWEDEN

054 DIANA DORADO
COLOMBIA

© Kristian Löveborg

055 THE SWEDISH SCHOOL
OF TEXTILES
SWEDEN

056 AMERICAN PÉREZ
SPAIN

057 A.F. VANDEVORST
BELGIUM

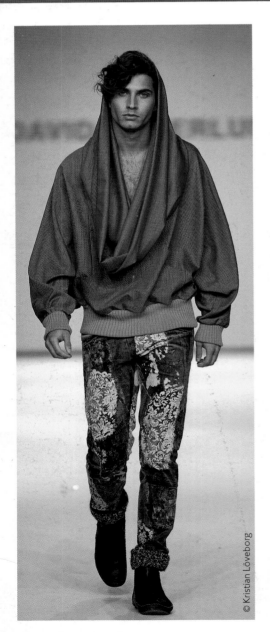

© Kristian Löveborg

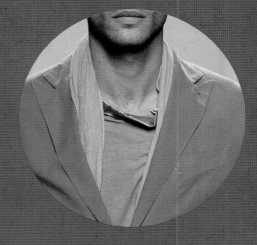

058 VICTORIO & LUCCHINO
SPAIN

059 CATI SERRÀ
SPAIN

060 VICTORIO & LUCCHINO
SPAIN

061 JEAN//PHILLIP
DENMARK

062 ALENA AKHMADULLINA
RUSSIA

063 EWA I WALLA
SWEDEN

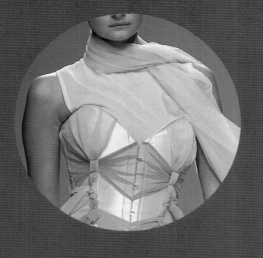

064 ELENA PRZHONSKAYA
UKRAINE

065 MAYA HANSEN
SPAIN

066 ELENA PRZHONSKAYA
UKRAINE

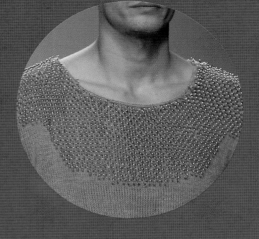

067 TSUMORI CHISATO
JAPAN

068 VASSILIOS KOSTETSOS
GREECE

069 CATI SERRÀ
SPAIN

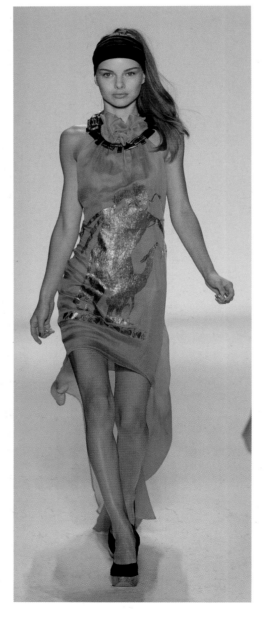

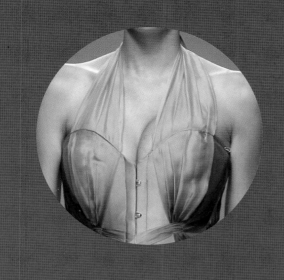

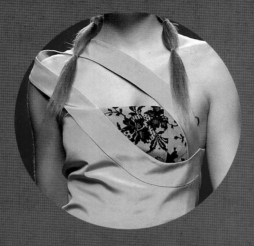

070 MAYA HANSEN
SPAIN

071 ANA LOCKING
SPAIN

072 NEREA LURGAIN
SPAIN

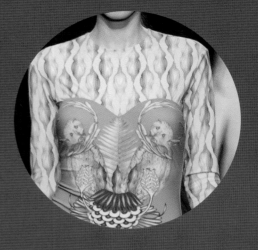

073   **MARTIN LAMOTHE**
SPAIN

074   **TSUMORI CHISATO**
JAPAN

075   **ALENA AKHMADULLINA**
RUSSIA

076 ALENA AKHMADULLINA
RUSSIA

077 NEREA LURGAIN
SPAIN

078 ALENA AKHMADULLINA
RUSSIA

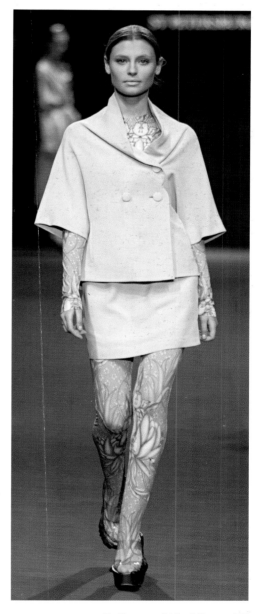

079 iON FIZ
SPAIN

080 AILANTO
SPAIN

081 MAL-AIMÉE
FRANCE

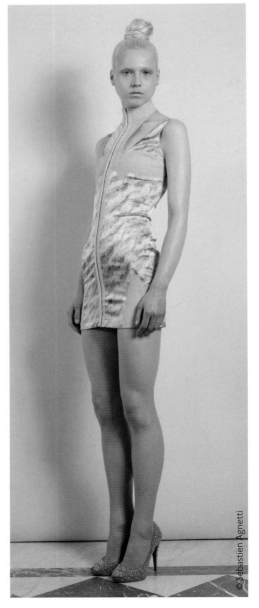

© Sébastien Agnetti

082 MAL-AIMÉE
FRANCE

083 ION FIZ
SPAIN

084 QASIMI
UNITED ARAB EMIRATES

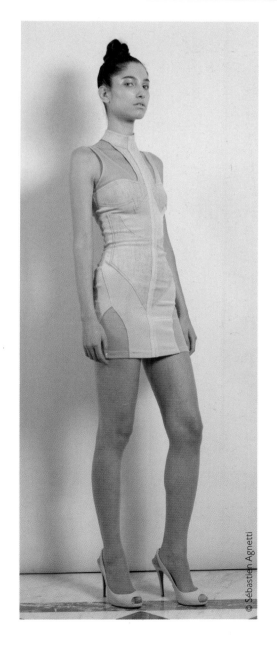

© Sébastien Agnetti

085 ALENA AKHMADULLINA
RUSSIA

086 DESIGNSKOLEN
KOLDING
DENMARK

087 STAS LOPATKIN
RUSSIA

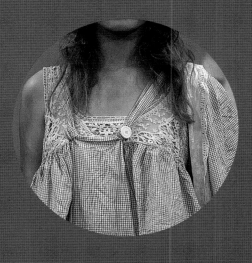

088 TSUMORI CHISATO
JAPAN

089 VICTORIO & LUCCHINO
SPAIN

090 EWA I WALLA
SWEDEN

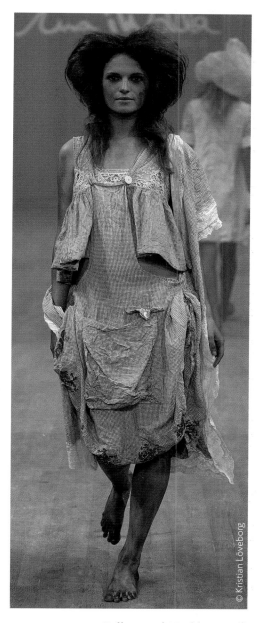

091 ERICA ZAIONTS
UKRAINE

092 QASIMI
UNITED ARAB EMIRATES

093 NEREA LURGAIN
SPAIN

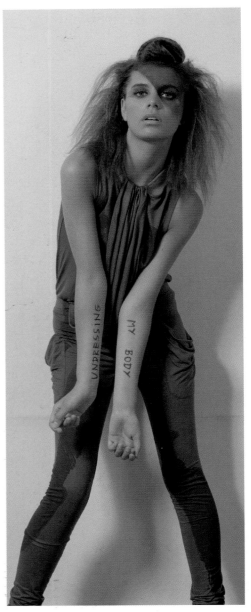

094 **DESIGNSKOLEN KOLDING**
DENMARK

095 **MANISH ARORA**
INDIA

096 **ERICA ZAIONTS**
UKRAINE

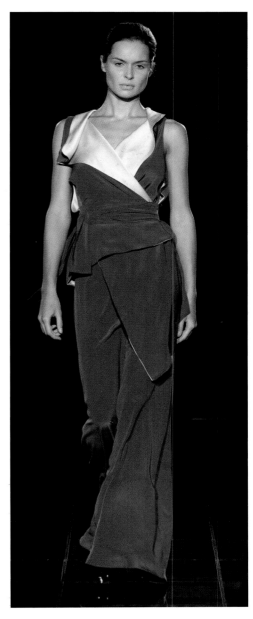

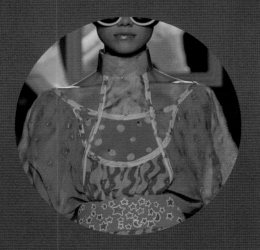

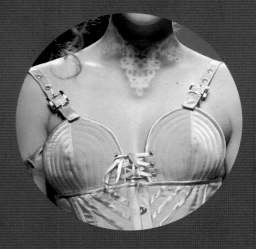

097 **TSUMORI CHISATO**
JAPAN

098 **ALENA AKHMADULLINA**
RUSSIA

099 **BIBIAN BLUE**
SPAIN

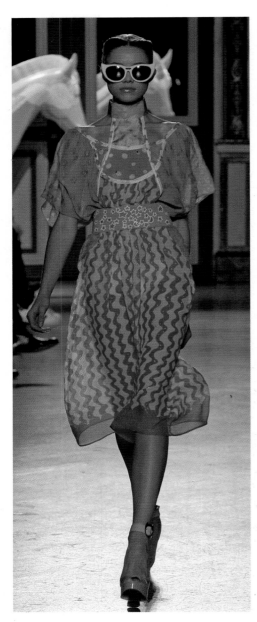

100 MALAFACHA BRAND
MEXICO

101 AGANOVICH
SERBIA/UK

102 ANNA MIMINOSHVILI
RUSSIA

103 LEMONIEZ
SPAIN

104 ANTONIO ALVARADO
SPAIN

105 BOHENTO
SPAIN

106 THE SWEDISH SCHOOL
OF TEXTILES
SWEDEN

107 DESIGNSKOLEN
KOLDING
DENMARK

108 ANTONIO ALVARADO
SPAIN

© Kristian Löveborg

Collars and Necklines **47**

109 BOHENTO
SPAIN

110 AILANTO
SPAIN

111 DIMITRI
ITALY

| 112 | THE SWEDISH SCHOOL OF TEXTILES SWEDEN | 113 | ANJARA SPAIN | 114 | DIMITRI ITALY |

© Kristian Löveborg

115 BOHENTO
SPAIN

116 A.F. VANDEVORST
BELGIUM

117 JEAN//PHILLIP
DENMARK

118 **JULIUS**
JAPAN

119 **A.F. VANDEVORST**
BELGIUM

120 **JEAN//PHILLIP**
DENMARK

© Étienne Tordoir

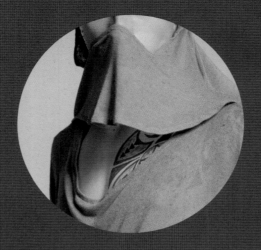

121 A.F. VANDEVORST
BELGIUM

122 ASHER LEVINE
USA

123 ALENA AKHMADULLINA
RUSSIA

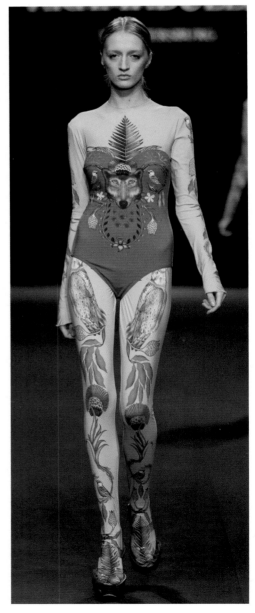

124 A.F. VANDEVORST
BELGIUM

125 SPIJKERS EN SPIJKERS
THE NETHERLANDS

126 THE SWEDISH SCHOOL
OF TEXTILES
SWEDEN

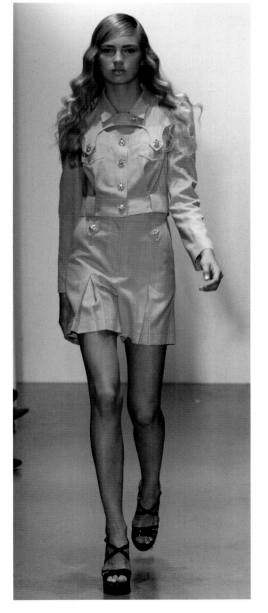

© Kristian Löveborg

127 DESIGNSKOLEN KOLDING DENMARK

128 JEAN//PHILLIP DENMARK

129 THE SWEDISH SCHOOL OF TEXTILES SWEDEN

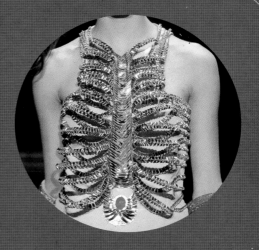

130 **BOHENTO**
SPAIN

131 **MALAFACHA BRAND**
MEXICO

132 **MANISH ARORA**
INDIA

133 J JS LEE
KOREA

134 BOHENTO
SPAIN

135 ALENA AKHMADULLINA
RUSSIA

136 MAYA HANSEN
SPAIN

137 J JS LEE
KOREA

138 IDA SJÖSTEDT
SWEDEN

© Kristian Löveborg

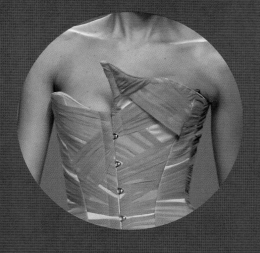

139 **MALAFACHA BRAND**
MEXICO

140 **ERICA ZAIONTS**
UKRAINE

141 **MAYA HANSEN**
SPAIN

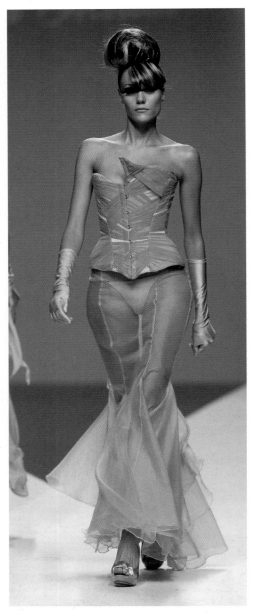

142   ANTONIO ALVARADO
SPAIN

143   MAL–AIMÉE
FRANCE

144   MAYA HANSEN
SPAIN

© Sébastien Agnetti

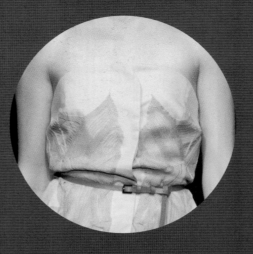

145 ASHER LEVINE
USA

146 ALENA AKHMADULLINA
RUSSIA

147 ELENA PRZHONSKAYA
UKRAINE

148 ASHER LEVINE
USA

149 CARLOS DÍEZ
SPAIN

150 ION FIZ
SPAIN

151 CAMILLA NORRBACK
FINLAND

152 SINPATRON
SPAIN

153 RICARDO DOURADO
PORTUGAL

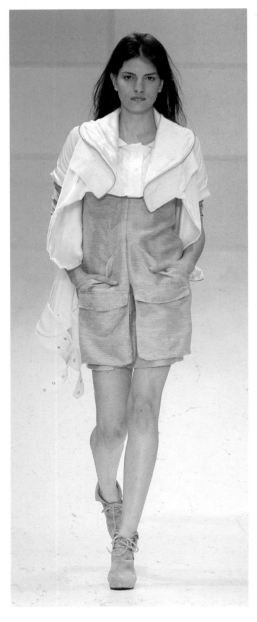

© Kristian Löveborg

154 EWA I WALLA
SWEDEN

155 KARLOTA LASPALAS
SPAIN

156 CAMILLA NORRBACK
FINLAND

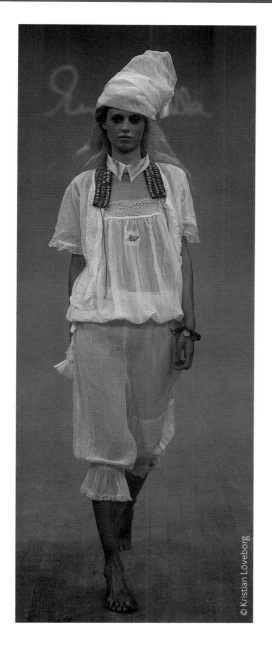

© Kristian Löveborg

© Kristian Löveborg

157 JULIUS
JAPAN

158 GEORGIA HARDINGE
UK

159 ERICA ZAIONTS
UKRAINE

© Étienne Tordoir

160 HARRIHALIM
INDONESIA

161 ASGER JUEL LARSEN
DENMARK

162 MARK FAST
CANADA

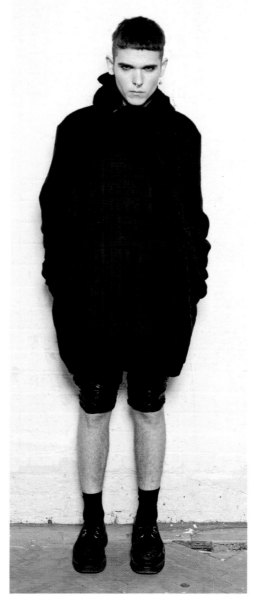

163 ANJARA
SPAIN

164 TSUMORI CHISATO
JAPAN

165 KRIS VAN ASSCHE
BELGIUM

166 QASIMI
UNITED ARAB EMIRATES

167 TSUMORI CHISATO
JAPAN

168 BORA AKSU
TURKEY

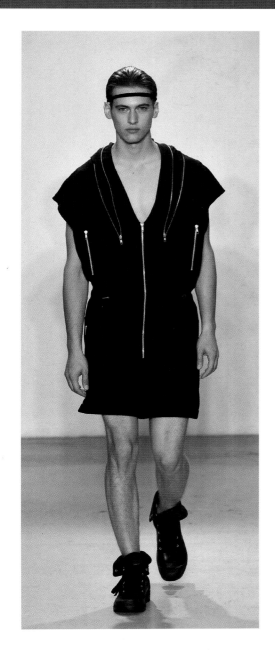

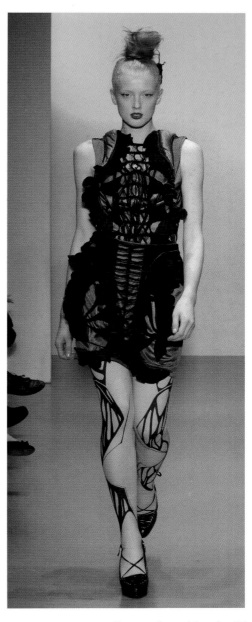

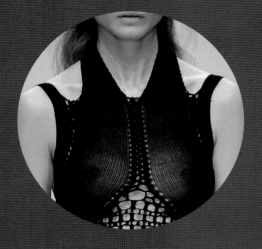

169 ANNA MIMINOSHVILI
RUSSIA

170 SPIJKERS EN SPIJKERS
THE NETHERLANDS

171 MARK FAST
CANADA

172 ERICA ZAIONTS
UKRAINE

173 HARRIHALIM
INDONESIA

174 ANNA MIMINOSHVILI
RUSSIA

175 **HARRIHALIM**
INDONESIA

176 **JULIUS**
JAPAN

177 **J JS LEE**
KOREA

178 ADA ZANDITON
UK

179 DESIGNSKOLEN
KOLDING
DENMARK

180 HARRIHALIM
INDONESIA

181 QASIMI
UNITED ARAB EMIRATES

182 HARRIHALIM
INDONESIA

183 THE SWEDISH SCHOOL
OF TEXTILES
SWEDEN

© Kristian Löveborg

184 **J JS LEE**
KOREA

185 **HARRIHALIM**
INDONESIA

186 **THE SWEDISH SCHOOL
OF TEXTILES**
SWEDEN

© Kristian Löveborg

187 MARK FAST
CANADA

188 TSUMORI CHISATO
JAPAN

189 TIM VAN STEENBERGEN
BELGIUM

© Étienne Tordoir

190   **MANISH ARORA**
INDIA

191   **VLADISLAV AKSENOV**
RUSSIA

192   **MARK FAST**
CANADA

Collars and Necklines   **75**

193 MARK FAST
CANADA

194 HARRIHALIM
INDONESIA

195 CAMILLA NORRBACK
FINLAND

© Kristian Löveborg

196 TSUMORI CHISATO
JAPAN

197 JULIUS
JAPAN

198 SPIJKERS EN SPIJKERS
THE NETHERLANDS

199 THE SWEDISH SCHOOL OF TEXTILES
SWEDEN

200 THE SWEDISH SCHOOL OF TEXTILES
SWEDEN

201 MARTA MONTOTO
SPAIN

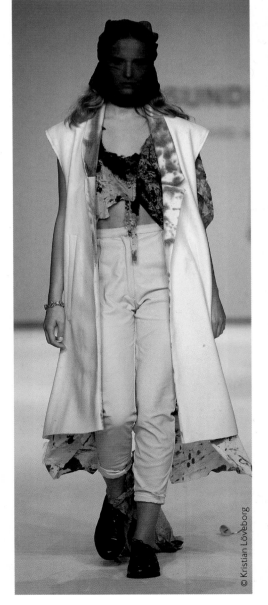

© Kristian Löveborg

© Kristian Löveborg

202 MALINI RAMANI
USA/INDIA

203 DESIGNSKOLEN
KOLDING
DENMARK

204 JULIUS
JAPAN

© Étienne Tordoir

205 KARLOTA LASPALAS
SPAIN

206 BORA AKSU
TURKEY

207 ELENA SKAKUN
RUSSIA

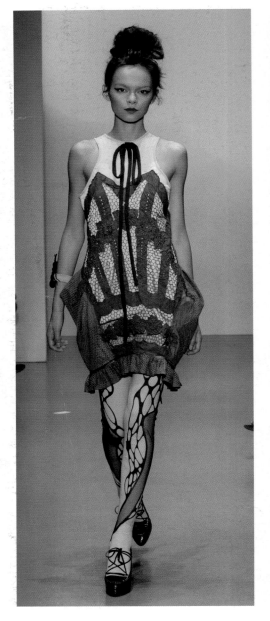

208 VLADISLAV AKSENOV
RUSSIA

209 ERICA ZAIONTS
UKRAINE

210 JEAN//PHILLIP
DENMARK

211   STAS LOPATKIN
RUSSIA

212   JEAN//PHILLIP
DENMARK

213   ANNA MIMINOSHVILI
RUSSIA

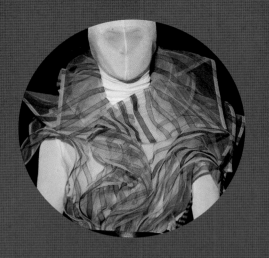

214 **ELENA SKAKUN**
RUSSIA

215 **JULIUS**
JAPAN

216 **ANNA MIMINOSHVILI**
RUSSIA

© Étienne Tordoir

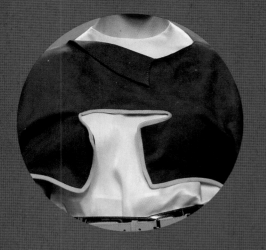

217 ION FIZ
SPAIN

218 TIM VAN STEENBERGEN
BELGIUM

219 SPIJKERS EN SPIJKERS
THE NETHERLANDS

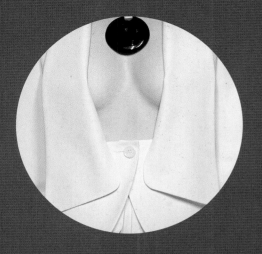

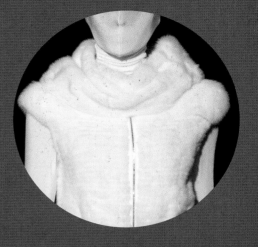

220 LEMONIEZ
SPAIN

221 AGANOVICH
SERBIA/UK

222 ELENA SKAKUN
RUSSIA

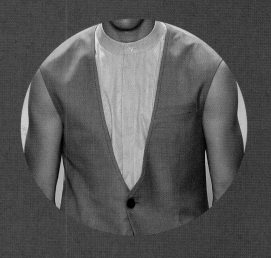

223 QASIMI
UNITED ARAB EMIRATES

224 JULIUS
JAPAN

225 VASSILIOS KOSTETSOS
GREECE

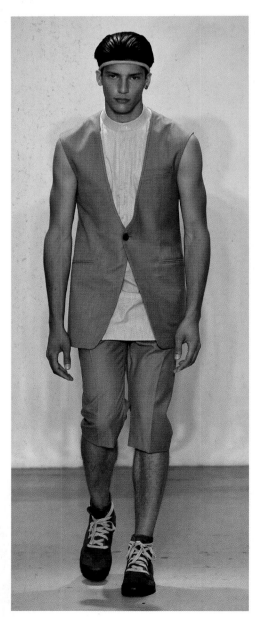

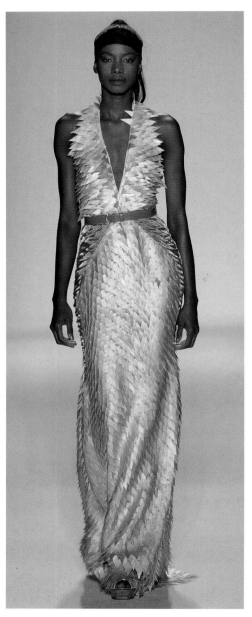

© Étienne Tordoir

226 QASIMI
UNITED ARAB EMIRATES

227 JULIUS
JAPAN

228 EWA I WALLA
SWEDEN

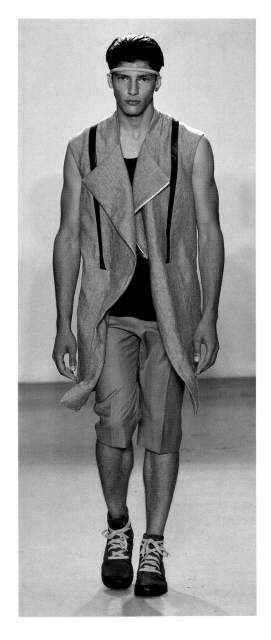

© Étienne Tordoir

© Kristian Löveborg

229 **ION FIZ**
SPAIN

230 **STAS LOPATKIN**
RUSSIA

231 **JULIUS**
JAPAN

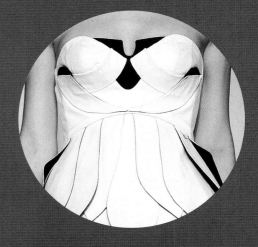

232 STAS LOPATKIN
RUSSIA

233 BIBIAN BLUE
SPAIN

234 ANNA MIMINOSHVILI
RUSSIA

235 JULIUS
JAPAN

236 DIANA DORADO
COLOMBIA

237 DAWID TOMASZEWSKI
POLAND

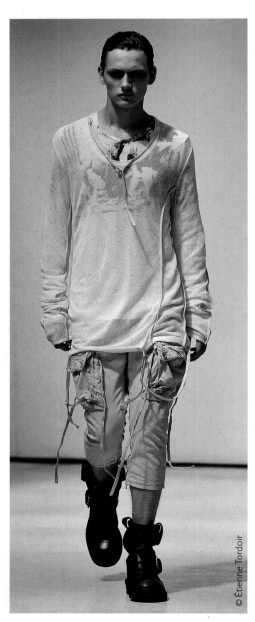
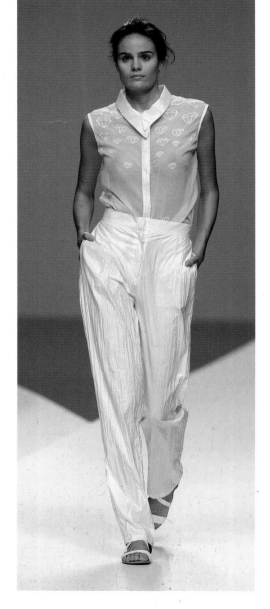

© Étienne Tordoir

© Mina Gerngross

238 MAL-AIMÉE
FRANCE

239 ANNA MIMINOSHVILI
RUSSIA

240 QASIMI
UNITED ARAB EMIRATES

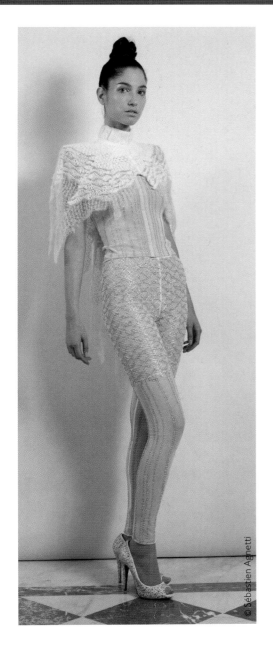

© Sébastien Agnetti

SHOULDERS AND SLEEVES

Shoulders and sleeves have a prominent role in current trends in fashion. After the subtlety and simplicity of the past two decades, runways around the world are now inundated with the spirit of the eighties with fashion proposals that concentrate the entire volume in this area, resulting in daring designs and creative concepts that convey richness and elegance. We include the legendary, exaggerated Grace Jones-style shoulder pads, whose revival this century is attributed to the French maison Balmain, along with so many others that border on an architectural interpretation, and those that remind us of samurai warrior armor. As for the sleeves, we see a considerable influence from this period, taking puffed, lantern, or gigot sleeves as a reference. Appliqués, epaulets, transparencies, structures, padding, and a countless number of techniques are included in the patterns of the most cutting-edge designs discussed in this chapter.

Vassilios Kostetsos. S/S 2011. MBFW New York.

241 ANJARA
SPAIN

242 THE SWEDISH SCHOOL
OF TEXTILES
SWEDEN

243 BORA AKSU
TURKEY

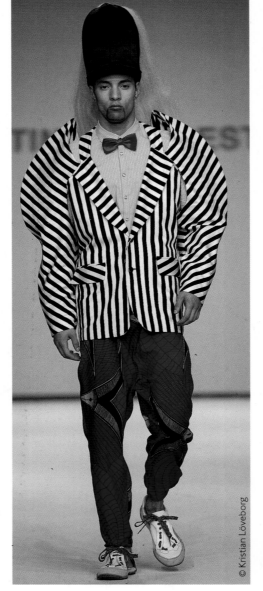

© Kristian Loveborg

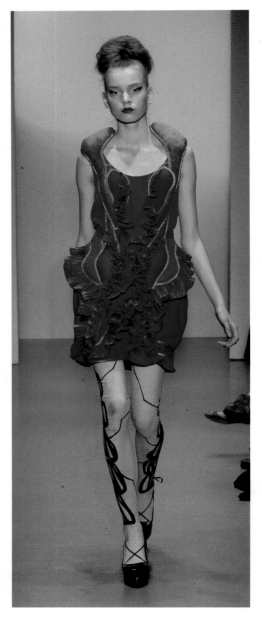

244 MALAFACHA BRAND
MEXICO

245 MANISH ARORA
INDIA

246 TSUMORI CHISATO
JAPAN

© Israel Esparza

© Yannis Vlamos

247 MALAFACHA BRAND
MEXICO

248 ANA LOCKING
SPAIN

249 ANA LOCKING
SPAIN

© Israel Esparza

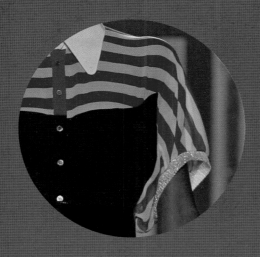
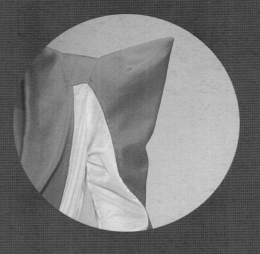

250 TSUMORI CHISATO
JAPAN

251 MALAFACHA BRAND
MEXICO

252 MANISH ARORA
INDIA

© Israel Esparza

© Yannis Vlamos

253 ANA LOCKING
SPAIN

254 SINPATRON
SPAIN

255 MALAFACHA BRAND
MEXICO

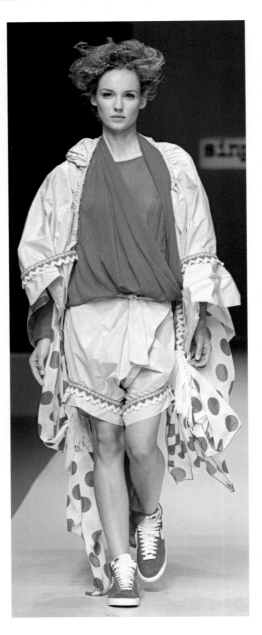

256 A.F. VANDEVORST
BELGIUM

257 MALAFACHA BRAND
MEXICO

258 ANTONIO ALVARADO
SPAIN

© Israel Esparza

259 THE SWEDISH SCHOOL OF TEXTILES
SWEDEN

260 ION FIZ
SPAIN

261 ELISA PALOMINO
SPAIN

© Kristian Löveborg

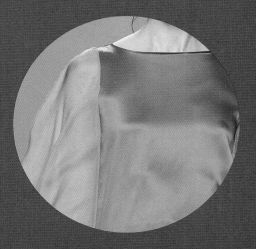

262 AGANOVICH
SERBIA/UK

263 DIMITRI
ITALY

264 VICTORIO & LUCCHINO
SPAIN

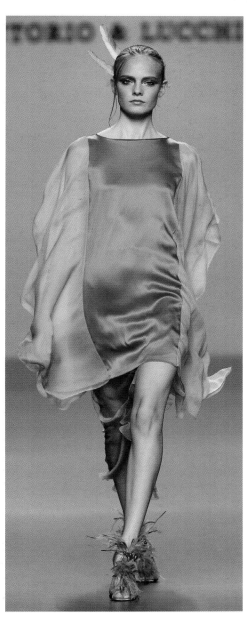

265 ANA LOCKING
SPAIN

266 G.V.G.V.
JAPAN

267 VASSILIOS KOSTETSOS
GREECE

268 G.V.G.V.
JAPAN

269 VASSILIOS KOSTETSOS
GREECE

270 THE SWEDISH SCHOOL
OF TEXTILES
SWEDEN

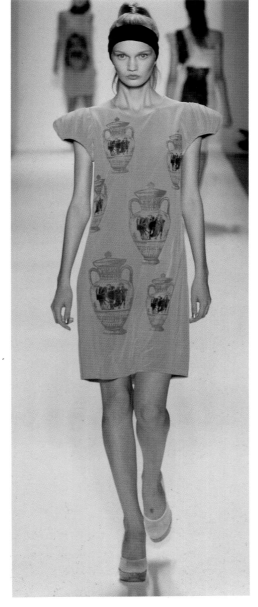

© Kristian Löveborg

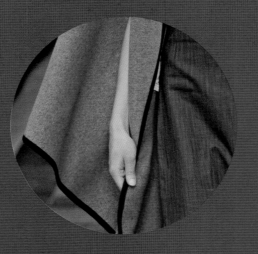

271 MALAFACHA BRAND
MEXICO

272 DESIGNSKOLEN
KOLDING
DENMARK

273 MANISH ARORA
INDIA

© Israel Esparza

© Yannis Vlamos

274 VASSILIOS KOSTETSOS
GREECE

275 DESIGNSKOLEN
KOLDING
DENMARK

276 BEBA'S CLOSET
SPAIN

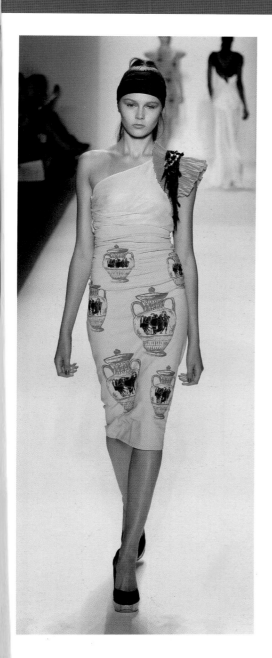

277 VASSILIOS KOSTETSOS
GREECE

278 DAWID TOMASZEWSKI
POLAND

279 ELENA PRZHONSKAYA
UKRAINE

© Mina Gerngross

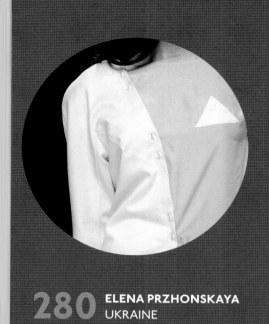

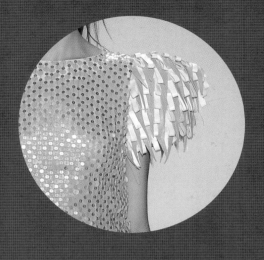

280 ELENA PRZHONSKAYA
UKRAINE

281 MARTIN LAMOTHE
SPAIN

282 VASSILIOS KOSTETSOS
GREECE

283 ANTONIO ALVARADO
SPAIN

284 ANTONIO ALVARADO
SPAIN

285 ALENA AKHMADULLINA
RUSSIA

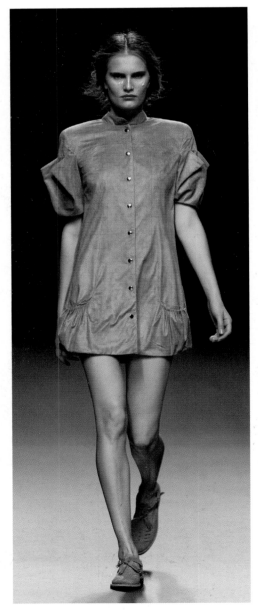

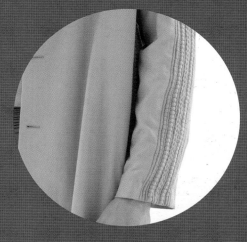

286 THE SWEDISH SCHOOL OF TEXTILES
SWEDEN

287 DESIGNSKOLEN KOLDING
DENMARK

288 EK THONGPRASERT
THAILAND

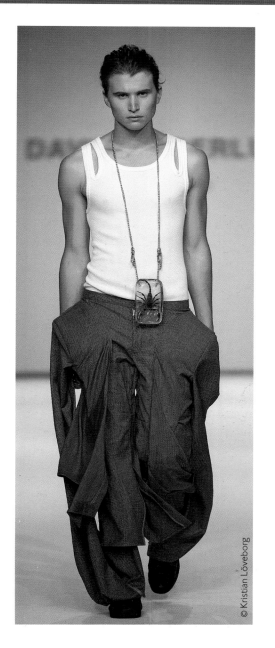

© Kristian Löveborg

289 ALI CHARISMA
INDONESIA

290 VASSILIOS KOSTETSOS
GREECE

291 MALINI RAMANI
USA/INDIA

292 ALI CHARISMA
INDONESIA

293 ALENA AKHMADULLINA
RUSSIA

294 MALINI RAMANI
USA/INDIA

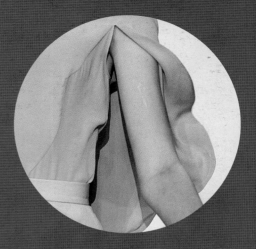

295 ELENA PRZHONSKAYA
UKRAINE

296 STAS LOPATKIN
RUSSIA

297 ANNA MIMINOSHVILI
RUSSIA

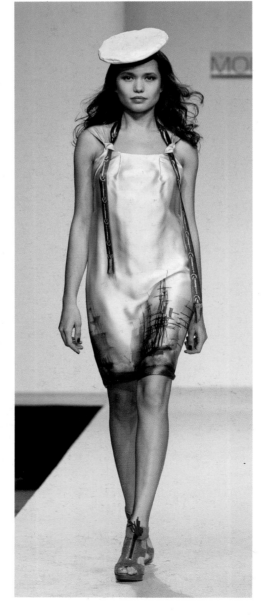

298 ELENA PRZHONSKAYA
UKRAINE

299 ANNA MIMINOSHVILI
RUSSIA

300 MAL-AIMÉE
FRANCE

© Sébastien Agnetti

301 CATI SERRÀ
SPAIN

302 MANISH ARORA
INDIA

303 ALENA AKHMADULLINA
RUSSIA

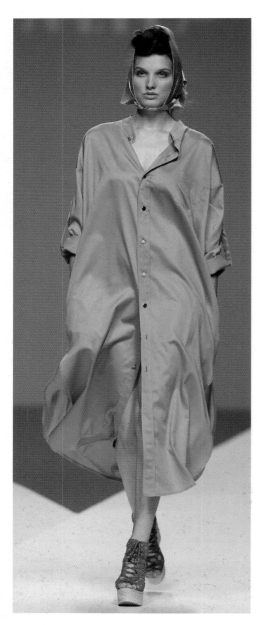

© Yannis.Vlamos

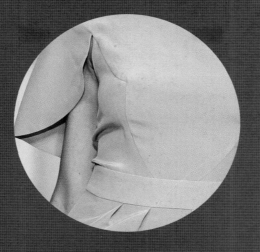

304 MANISH ARORA
INDIA

305 ANNA MIMINOSHVILI
RUSSIA

306 MANISH ARORA
INDIA

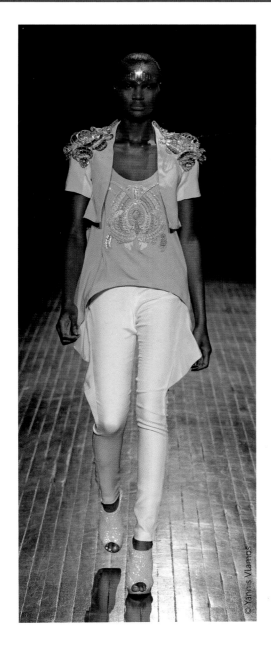

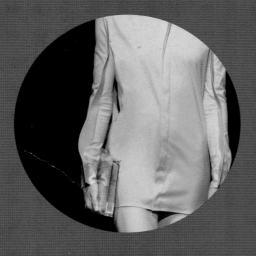

307 VASSILIOS KOSTETSOS
GREECE

308 MAISON MARTIN
MARGIELA
FRANCE

309 MAL-AIMÉE
FRANCE

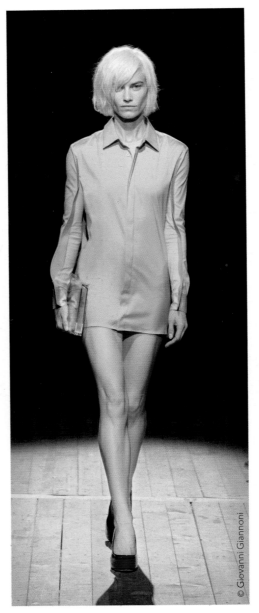

310 MAL-AIMÉE
FRANCE

311 AMERICAN PÉREZ
SPAIN

312 GEORGIA HARDINGE
UK

© Sébastien Agnetti

313 **DESIGNSKOLEN KOLDING** DENMARK

314 **DESIGNSKOLEN KOLDING** DENMARK

315 **CAMILLA NORRBACK** FINLAND

© Kristian Löveborg

316 MALAFACHA BRAND
MEXICO

317 VASSILIOS KOSTETSOS
GREECE

318 DESIGNSKOLEN
KOLDING
DENMARK

© Israel Esparza

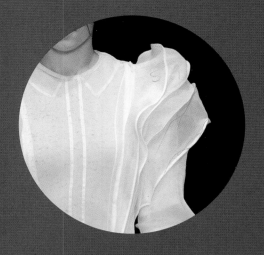

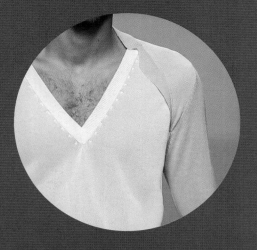

319 DESIGNSKOLEN
KOLDING
DENMARK

320 ION FIZ
SPAIN

321 IDA SJÖSTEDT
SWEDEN

© Kristian Löveborg

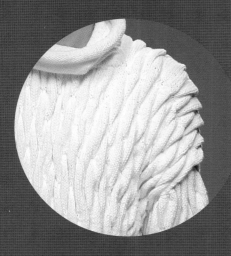

322 CATI SERRÀ
SPAIN

323 GEORGIA HARDINGE
UK

324 STAS LOPATKIN
RUSSIA

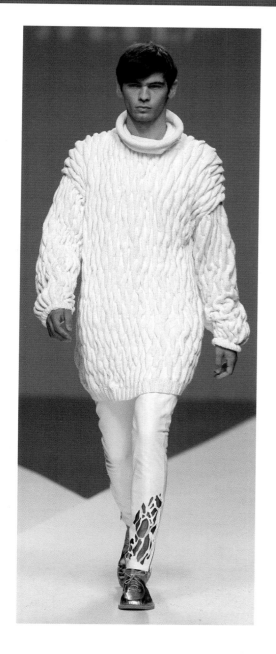

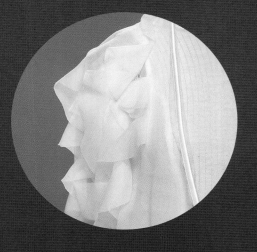
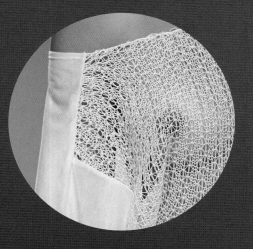

325 ASHER LEVINE
USA

326 DIANA DORADO
COLOMBIA

327 CATI SERRÀ
SPAIN

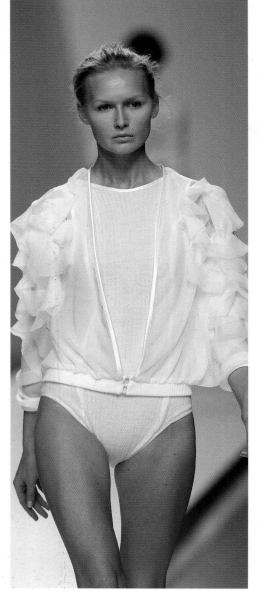

328 ION FIZ
SPAIN

329 THE SWEDISH SCHOOL
OF TEXTILES
SWEDEN

330 VASSILIOS KOSTETSOS
GREECE

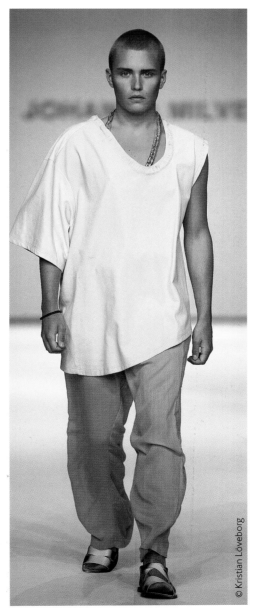

© Kristian Löveborg

331 BEBA'S CLOSET
SPAIN

332 DESIGNSKOLEN
KOLDING
DENMARK

333 CAMILLA NORRBACK
FINLAND

© Kristian Löveborg

334 MAL-AIMÉE
FRANCE

335 BEBA'S CLOSET
SPAIN

336 DESIGNSKOLEN
KOLDING
DENMARK

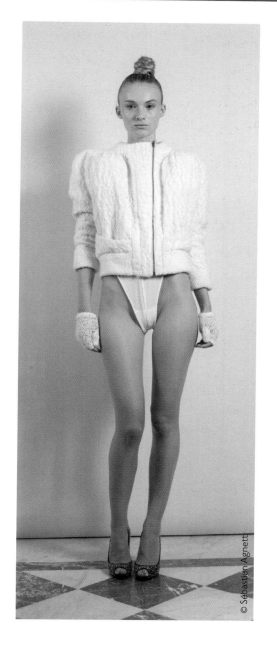

© Sébastien Agnetti

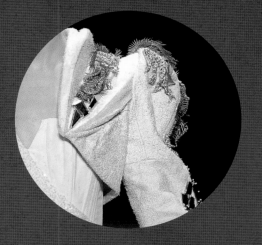 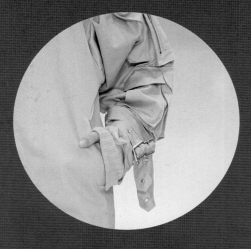 

337   MANISH ARORA
INDIA

338   RICARDO DOURADO
PORTUGAL

339   VASSILIOS KOSTETSOS
GREECE

© Yannis Vlamos

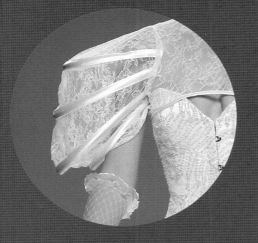
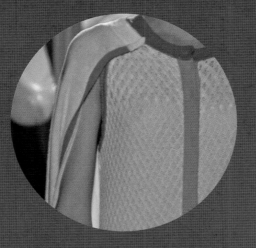

340 MAYA HANSEN
SPAIN

341 TSUMORI CHISATO
JAPAN

342 ALI CHARISMA
INDONESIA

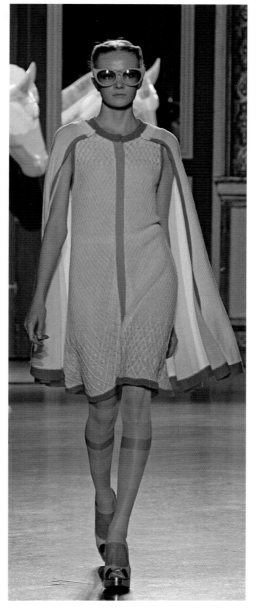

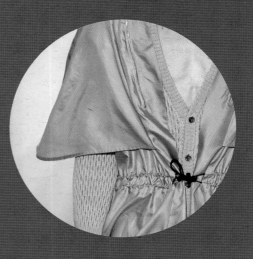

343 DESIGNSKOLEN KOLDING
DENMARK

344 THE SWEDISH SCHOOL OF TEXTILES
SWEDEN

345 QASIMI
UNITED ARAB EMIRATES

© Kristian Löveborg

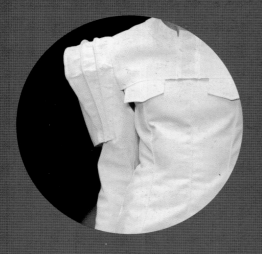

346 **DESIGNSKOLEN KOLDING** DENMARK

347 **JEAN//PHILLIP** DENMARK

348 **MAL-AIMÉE** FRANCE

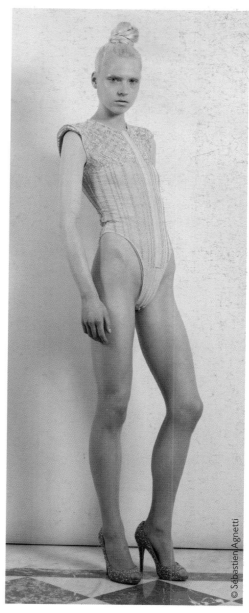

© Sébastien Agnetti

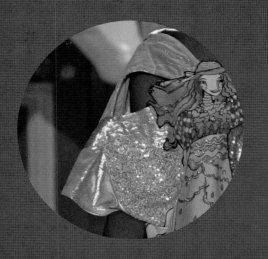

349 TSUMORI CHISATO
JAPAN

350 QASIMI
UNITED ARAB EMIRATES

351 SINPATRON
SPAIN

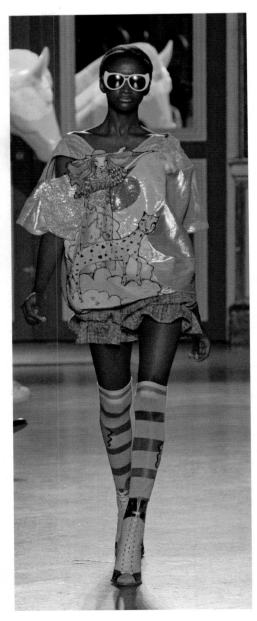

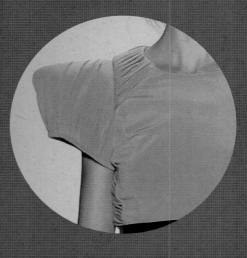

352 VASSILIOS KOSTETSOS
GREECE

353 IDA SJÖSTEDT
SWEDEN

354 VASSILIOS KOSTETSOS
GREECE

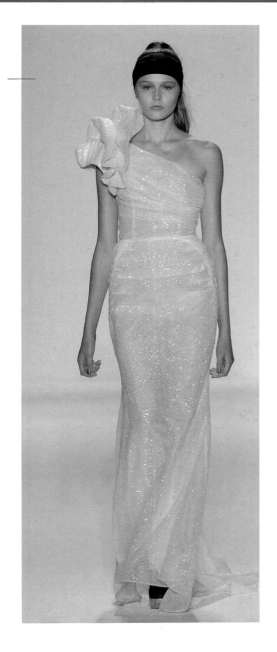

© Kristian Löveborg

355 JEAN//PHILLIP
DENMARK

356 QASIMI
UNITED ARAB EMIRATES

357 VRL COLLECTION
SPAIN

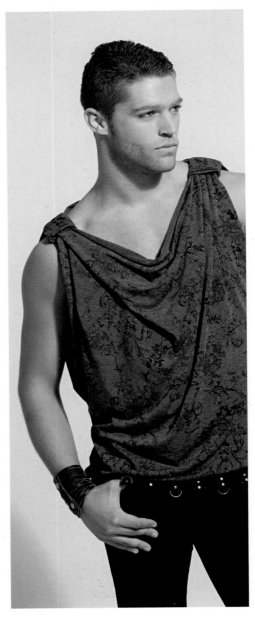

358 VLADISLAV AKSENOV
RUSSIA

359 VRL COLLECTION
SPAIN

360 ASHER LEVINE
USA

361 DESIGNSKOLEN KOLDING
DENMARK

362 ASHER LEVINE
USA

363 DESIGNSKOLEN KOLDING
DENMARK

364 VASSILIOS KOSTETSOS
GREECE

365 DIMITRI
ITALY

366 BERNARD CHANDRAN
MALAYSIA

367 IDA SJÖSTEDT
SWEDEN

368 VASSILIOS KOSTETSOS
GREECE

369 TIM VAN STEENBERGEN
BELGIUM

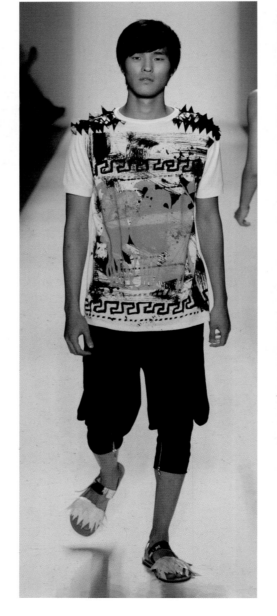

© Kristian Löveborg

© Étienne Tordoir

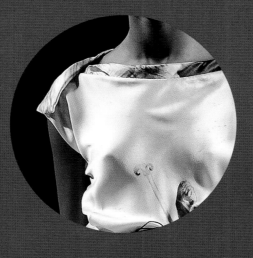

370 THE SWEDISH SCHOOL
OF TEXTILES
SWEDEN

371 TIM VAN STEENBERGEN
BELGIUM

372 SPIJKERS EN SPIJKERS
THE NETHERLANDS

© Kristian Löveborg

© Étienne Tordoir

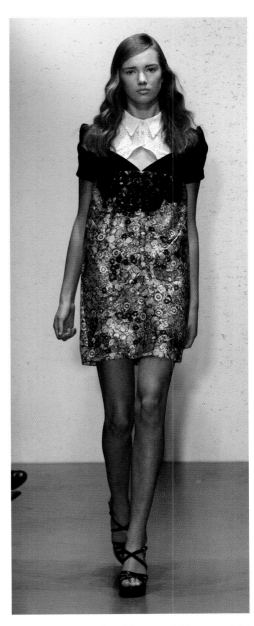

373 THE SWEDISH SCHOOL
OF TEXTILES
SWEDEN

374 TSUMORI CHISATO
JAPAN

375 EWA I WALLA
SWEDEN

© Kristian Löveborg

© Kristian Löveborg

376 TSUMORI CHISATO
JAPAN

377 ELISA PALOMINO
SPAIN

378 ALI CHARISMA
INDONESIA

Shoulders and Sleeves **139**

379 TSUMORI CHISATO
JAPAN

380 AGANOVICH
SERBIA/UK

381 ELENA SKAKUN
RUSSIA

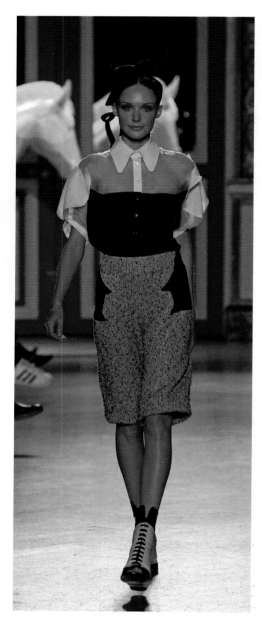

382 SPIJKERS EN SPIJKERS
THE NETHERLANDS

383 VASSILIOS KOSTETSOS
GREECE

384 AGANOVICH
SERBIA/UK

385 BIBIAN BLUE
SPAIN

386 STAS LOPATKIN
RUSSIA

387 MAYA HANSEN
SPAIN

388 DAWID TOMASZEWSKI
POLAND

389 BIBIAN BLUE
SPAIN

390 VASSILIOS KOSTETSOS
GREECE

© Mina Gerngross

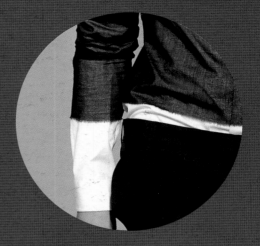

391 DESIGNSKOLEN KOLDING
DENMARK

392 ANJARA
SPAIN

393 KRIS VAN ASSCHE
BELGIUM

© Patrice Stable

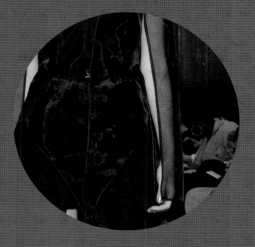

394 MAL-AIMÉE
FRANCE

395 HARRIHALIM
INDONESIA

396 DESIGNSKOLEN
KOLDING
DENMARK

© Sébastien Agnetti

Shoulders and Sleeves **145**

397 AILANTO
SPAIN

398 MARK FAST
CANADA

399 GEORGIA HARDINGE
UK

400 MARCEL OSTERTAG
GERMANY

401 QASIMI
UNITED ARAB EMIRATES

402 BERNARD CHANDRAN
MALAYSIA

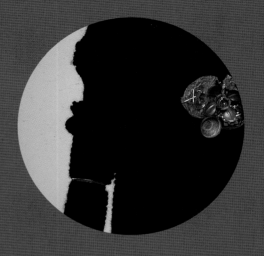

403 RICARDO DOURADO
PORTUGAL

404 CHARLIE LE MINDU
FRANCE

405 THE SWEDISH SCHOOL
OF TEXTILES
SWEDEN

406 TSUMORI CHISATO
JAPAN

407 VLADISLAV AKSENOV
RUSSIA

408 ALI CHARISMA
INDONESIA

409 HARRIHALIM
INDONESIA

410 DESIGNSKOLEN
KOLDING
DENMARK

411 ANNA MIMINOSHVILI
RUSSIA

412 VRL COLLECTION
SPAIN

413 TIM VAN STEENBERGEN
BELGIUM

414 DESIGNSKOLEN
KOLDING
DENMARK

© Étienne Tordoir

WAISTLINES

The waistline is paramount when designing garments. Determining the shape and design of the waistline also determines the silhouette of a look. The use of waistbands causes an illusory effect in many cases: when it is not in line with the actual position of the waist, and it lies either above or below it, it can visually lengthen the legs, enhance the bust, or highlight the hips. This chapter shows the different details and shapes used by designers in this area to enhance both the female and male figure. Some reference the forties, with very high waistlines that stylize the figure. Other models invoke the fifties, where the waist is defined in a more marked manner, balancing out the figure evenly between the hip and bust, Marilyn-style. Low waistlines, gathers, appliqués, seams, sashes, corsets, and belts complement and highlight the waistbands that are featured in this book.

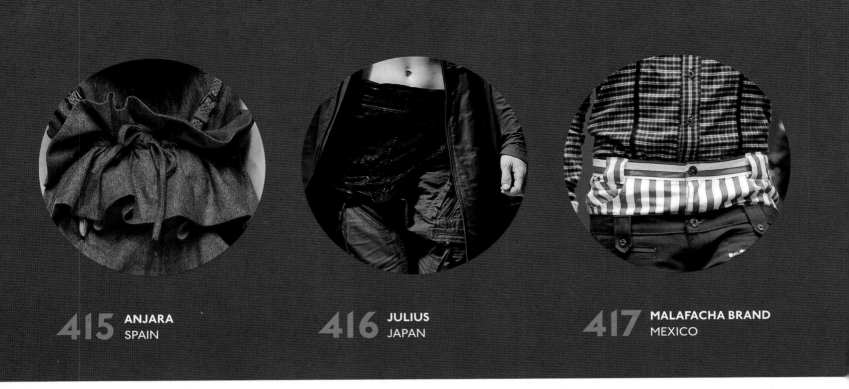

415 ANJARA
SPAIN

416 JULIUS
JAPAN

417 MALAFACHA BRAND
MEXICO

© Étienne Tordoir

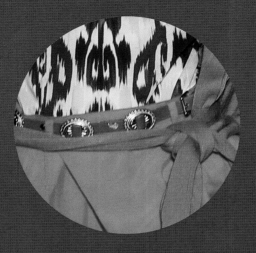
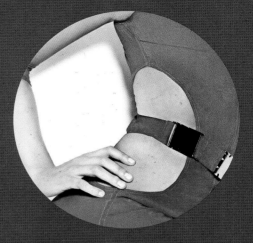

418 MARCEL OSTERTAG
GERMANY

419 G.V.G.V.
JAPAN

420 HASAN HEJAZI
UK

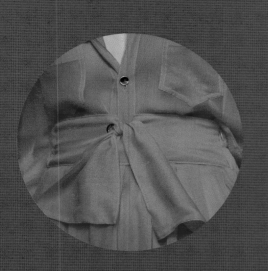

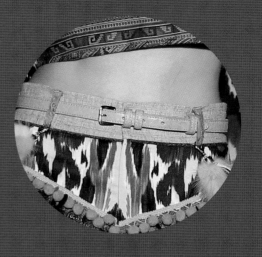

421 CATI SERRÀ
SPAIN

422 THE SWEDISH SCHOOL
OF TEXTILES
SWEDEN

423 G.V.G.V.
JAPAN

© Kristian Loveborg

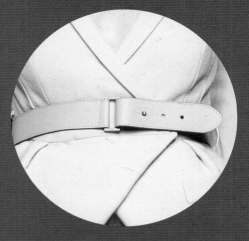

424 MARCEL OSTERTAG
GERMANY

425 THE SWEDISH SCHOOL
OF TEXTILES
SWEDEN

426 ANA LOCKING
SPAIN

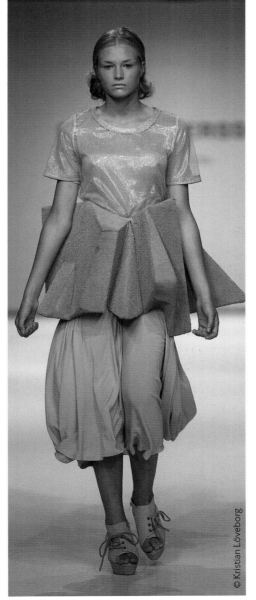

© Kristian Löveborg

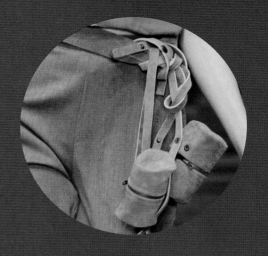

427 DESIGNSKOLEN KOLDING
DENMARK

428 G.V.G.V.
JAPAN

429 DESIGNSKOLEN KOLDING
DENMARK

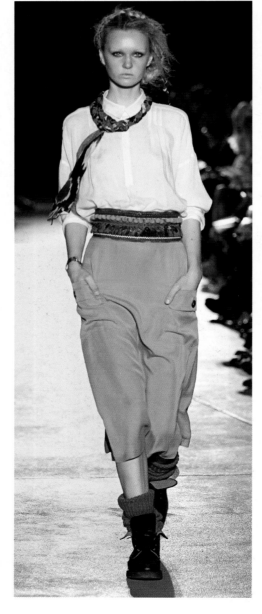

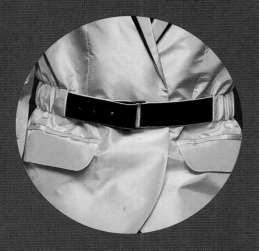

430 ANA LOCKING
SPAIN

431 MALAFACHA BRAND
MEXICO

432 ANA LOCKING
SPAIN

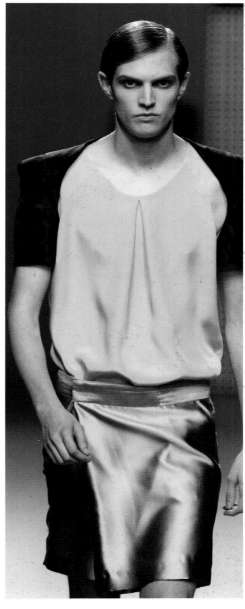

© Israel Esparza

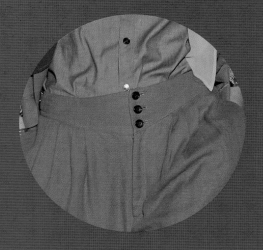

433 DIMITRI
ITALY

434 MALAFACHA BRAND
MEXICO

435 G.V.G.V.
JAPAN

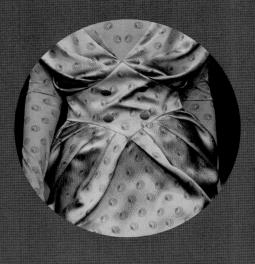

436 CATI SERRÀ
SPAIN

437 ALENA AKHMADULLINA
RUSSIA

438 BOHENTO
SPAIN

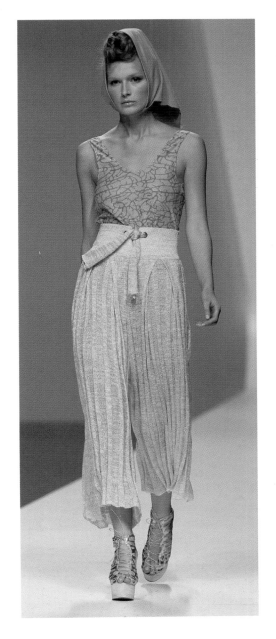
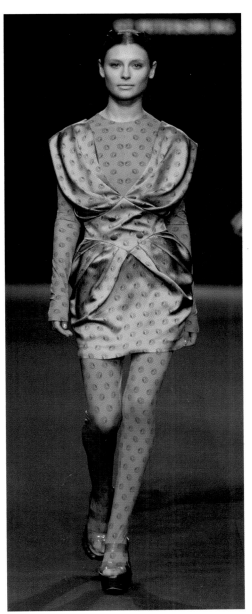

439 ANJARA
SPAIN

440 EWA I WALLA
SWEDEN

441 ERICA ZAIONTS
UKRAINE

© Kristian Löveborg

442 MALAFACHA BRAND
MEXICO

443 MAISON MARTIN
MARGIELA
FRANCE

444 ALI CHARISMA
INDONESIA

© Giovanni Giannoni

445 ERICA ZAIONTS
UKRAINE

446 ANNA MIMINOSHVILI
RUSSIA

447 MAL-AIMÉE
FRANCE

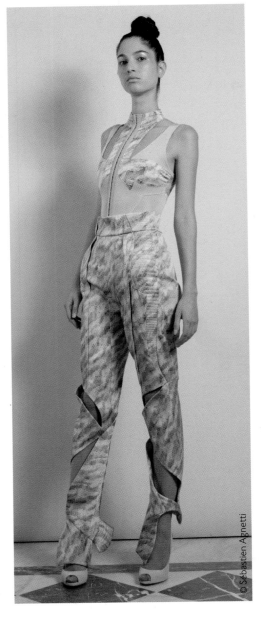

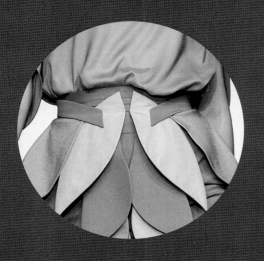

448 ANNA MIMINOSHVILI
RUSSIA

449 MANISH ARORA
INDIA

450 RICARDO DOURADO
PORTUGAL

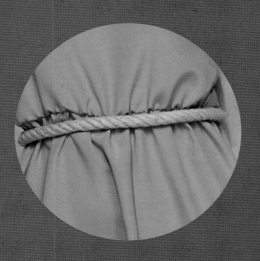
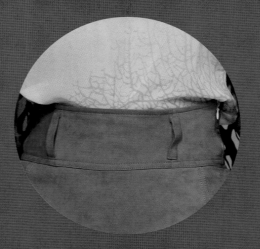

451 BEBA'S CLOSET
SPAIN

452 CATI SERRÀ
SPAIN

453 CATI SERRÀ
SPAIN

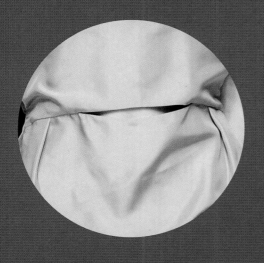

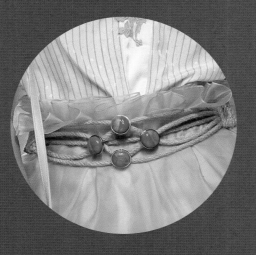

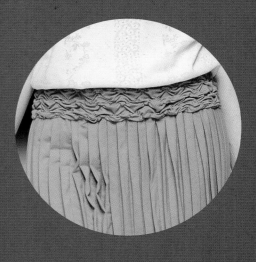

454 **ELENA PRZHONSKAYA**
UKRAINE

455 **BEBA'S CLOSET**
SPAIN

456 **ELENA PRZHONSKAYA**
UKRAINE

457 DESIGNSKOLEN KOLDING
DENMARK

458 EK THONGPRASERT
THAILAND

459 DESIGNSKOLEN KOLDING
DENMARK

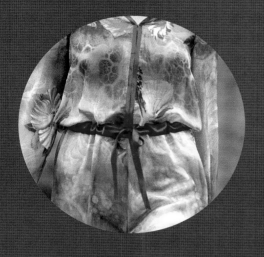

460 IDA SJÖSTEDT
SWEDEN

461 ASHER LEVINE
USA

462 AILANTO
SPAIN

© Kristian Löveborg

463 JEAN//PHILLIP
DENMARK

464 BOHENTO
SPAIN

465 RICARDO DOURADO
PORTUGAL

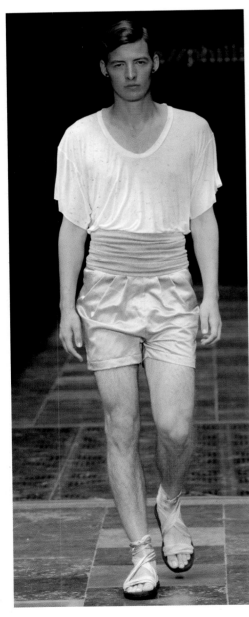

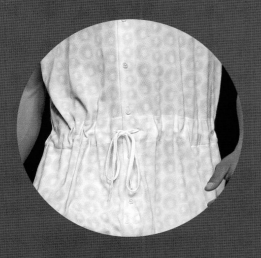

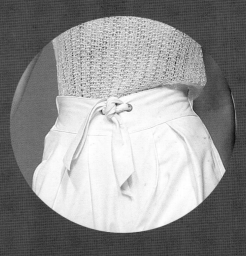

466 CARLOS DÍEZ
SPAIN

467 EWA I WALLA
SWEDEN

468 CATI SERRÀ
SPAIN

© Kristian Löveborg

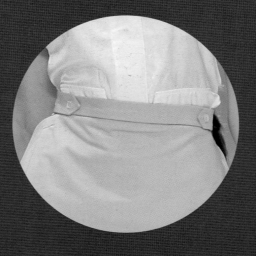

469 JEAN//PHILLIP
DENMARK

470 RICARDO DOURADO
PORTUGAL

471 AILANTO
SPAIN

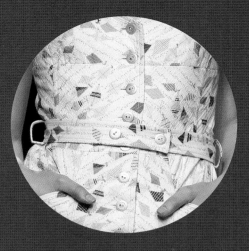

472 EWA I WALLA
SWEDEN

473 CAMILLA NORRBACK
FINLAND

474 AILANTO
SPAIN

© Kristian Löveborg

475 KRIS VAN ASSCHE
BELGIUM

476 DESIGNSKOLEN
KOLDING
DENMARK

477 EK THONGPRASERT
THAILAND

© Patrice Stable

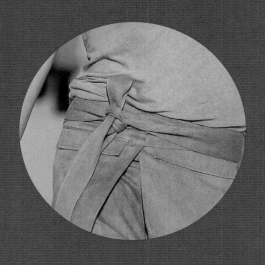

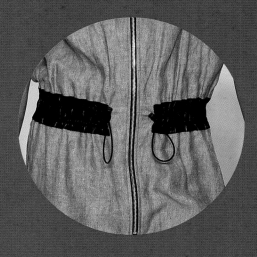

478   **KRIS VAN ASSCHE**
BELGIUM

479   **NEREA LURGAIN**
SPAIN

480   **QASIMI**
UNITED ARAB EMIRATES

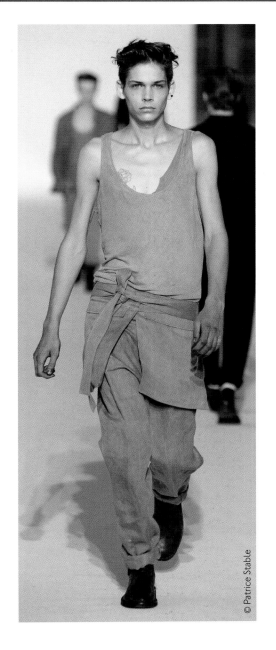

© Patrice Stable

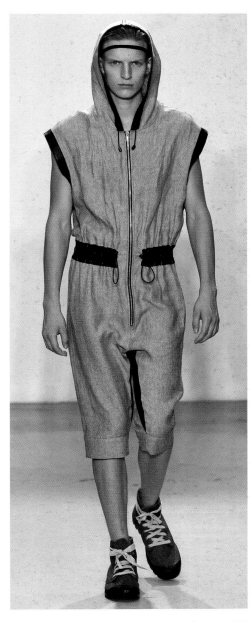

481 ASHER LEVINE
USA

482 AILANTO
SPAIN

483 ANNA MIMINOSHVILI
RUSSIA

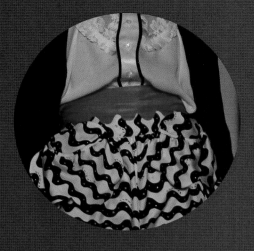

484 TIM VAN STEENBERGEN
BELGIUM

485 VLADISLAV AKSENOV
RUSSIA

486 TSUMORI CHISATO
JAPAN

© Étienne Tordoir

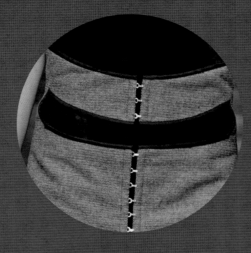

487 KRIS VAN ASSCHE
BELGIUM

488 DESIGNSKOLEN
KOLDING
DENMARK

489 ELENA SKAKUN
RUSSIA

© Patrice Stable

490 ERICA ZAIONTS
UKRAINE

491 JEAN//PHILLIP
DENMARK

492 STAS LOPATKIN
RUSSIA

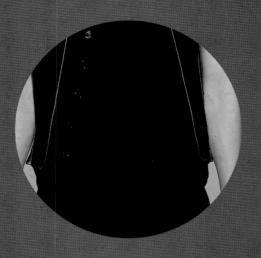

493 KRIS VAN ASSCHE
BELGIUM

494 HARRIHALIM
INDONESIA

495 JEAN//PHILLIP
DENMARK

© Patrice Stable

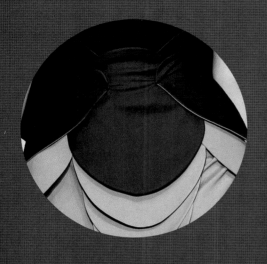

496 ANNA MIMINOSHVILI
RUSSIA

497 JULIUS
JAPAN

498 TIM VAN STEENBERGEN
BELGIUM

© Étienne Tordoir

© Étienne Tordoir

499 ERICA ZAIONTS
UKRAINE

500 THE SWEDISH SCHOOL
OF TEXTILES
SWEDEN

501 SPIJKERS EN SPIJKERS
THE NETHERLANDS

© Kristian Löveborg

502 AILANTO
SPAIN

503 ERICA ZAIONTS
UKRAINE

504 ELENA PRZHONSKAYA
UKRAINE

POCKETS, ZIPPERS, AND BUTTONS

This section compiles together different details that primarily had a practical use and that currently, in many cases, have a decorative role: pockets, buttons, snap rings, bundles, zippers, hooks, clips, Velcro, and buckles. Many of these started off as working or military accessories, however because of their functionality they were incorporated into civilian clothes and consequently into current fashion trends. Perhaps the zipper is the accessory that has evolved the most, invented by Gideon Sundback in 1913 and patented in 1917 as a "hookless fastener." In 1923, the Goodrich Corporation coined the onomatopoeic name "zipper." Today there are a wide variety of zippers on the market, including waterproof and invisible zippers, and they are available in materials such as polyester or metal alloys. We will see how the influence of zippers on eighties-style leather jackets is very much present in fashion today, giving many looks a more punk and rock style.

Karlota Laspalas. S/S 2011. 080 Barcelona Fashion Week.

505 ANJARA
SPAIN

506 ANTONIO ALVARADO
SPAIN

507 MARCEL OSTERTAG
GERMANY

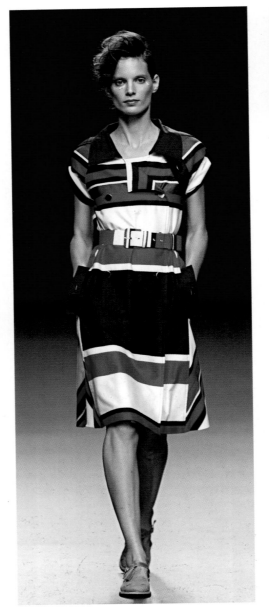

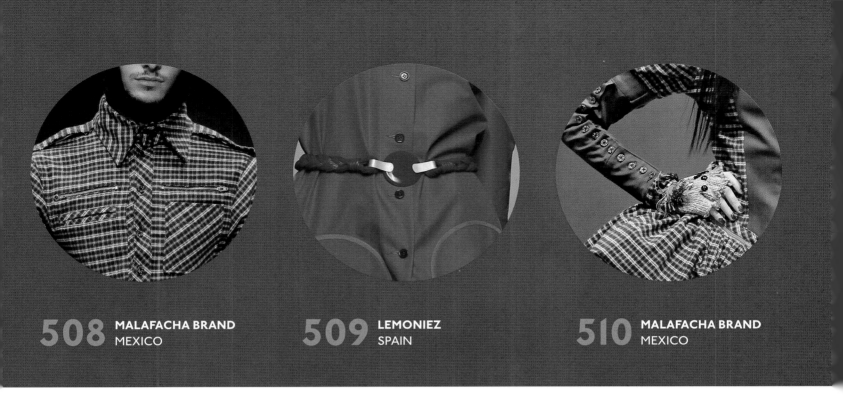

508 MALAFACHA BRAND
MEXICO

509 LEMONIEZ
SPAIN

510 MALAFACHA BRAND
MEXICO

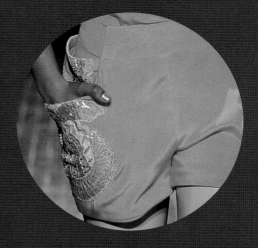

511 SPIJKERS EN SPIJKERS
THE NETHERLANDS

512 MALAFACHA BRAND
MEXICO

513 MANISH ARORA
INDIA

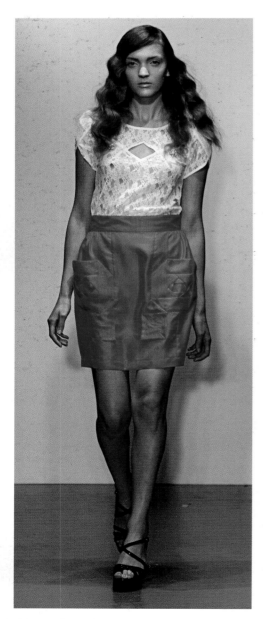

514 MALAFACHA BRAND
MEXICO

515 AILANTO
SPAIN

516 MALAFACHA BRAND
MEXICO

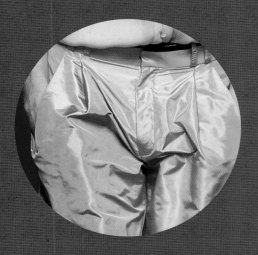

517 ANA LOCKING
SPAIN

518 ALENA AKHMADULLINA
RUSSIA

519 MARTIN LAMOTHE
SPAIN

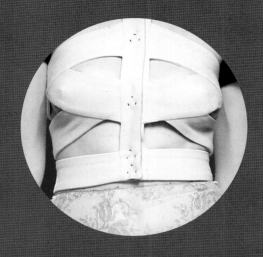

520 ANA LOCKING
SPAIN

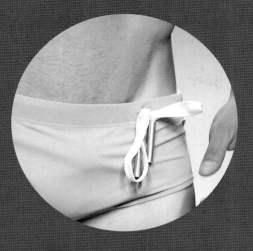

521 ANTONIO ALVARADO
SPAIN

522 CATI SERRÀ
SPAIN

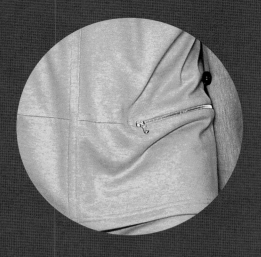

523 QASIMI
UNITED ARAB EMIRATES

524 CARLOS DÍEZ
SPAIN

525 DESIGNSKOLEN
KOLDING
DENMARK

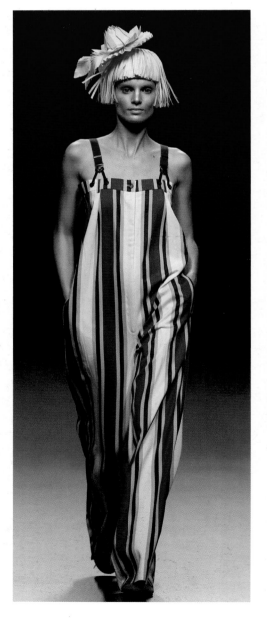

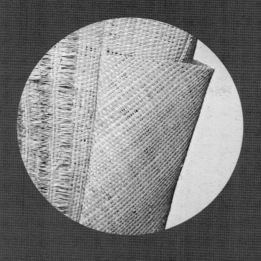

526   **ALENA AKHMADULLINA**
RUSSIA

527   **MARTIN LAMOTHE**
SPAIN

528   **DESIGNSKOLEN KOLDING**
DENMARK

529 EWA I WALLA
SWEDEN

530 JEAN//PHILLIP
DENMARK

531 KARLOTA LASPALAS
SPAIN

© Kristian Löveborg

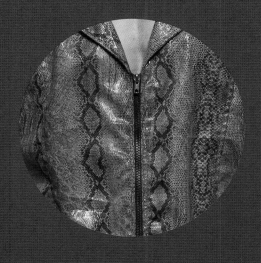

532 ANTONIO ALVARADO
SPAIN

533 KARLOTA LASPALAS
SPAIN

534 THE SWEDISH SCHOOL
OF TEXTILES
SWEDEN

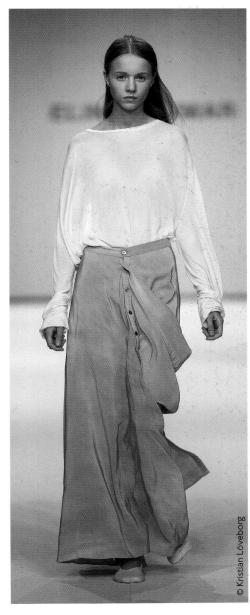

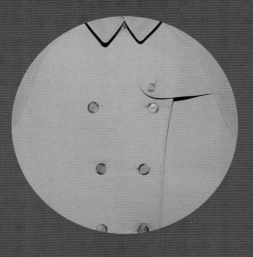

535 ELENA PRZHONSKAYA
UKRAINE

536 MAISON MARTIN
MARGIELA
FRANCE

537 JEAN//PHILLIP
DENMARK

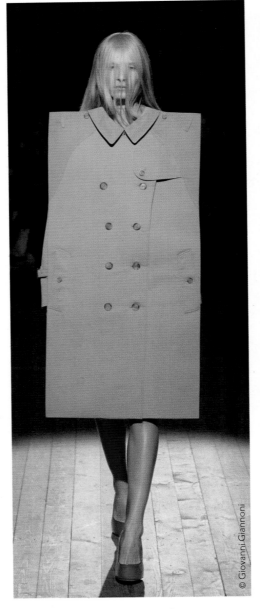

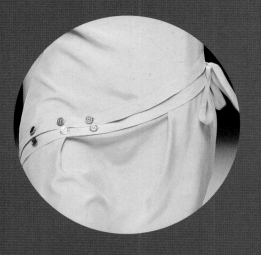

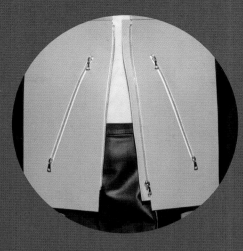

538 ELENA PRZHONSKAYA
UKRAINE

539 MAISON MARTIN
MARGIELA
FRANCE

540 JEAN//PHILLIP
DENMARK

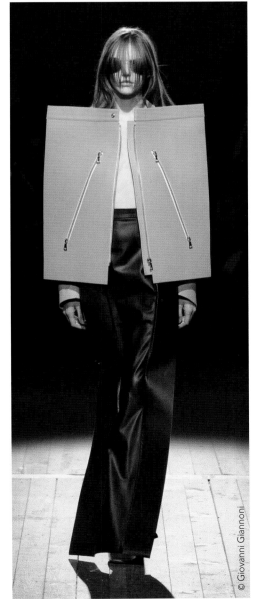

© Giovanni Giannoni

541 HASAN HEJAZI
UK

542 RICARDO DOURADO
PORTUGAL

543 RICARDO DOURADO
PORTUGAL

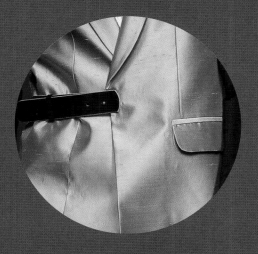

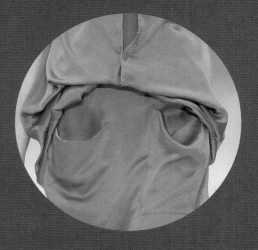

544 DESIGNSKOLEN KOLDING
DENMARK

545 ANA LOCKING
SPAIN

546 RICARDO DOURADO
PORTUGAL

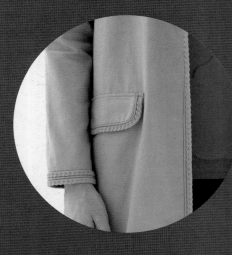

547 ALENA AKHMADULLINA
RUSSIA

548 EK THONGPRASERT
THAILAND

549 DESIGNSKOLEN
KOLDING
DENMARK

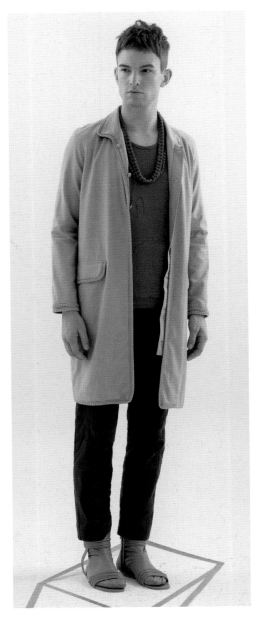

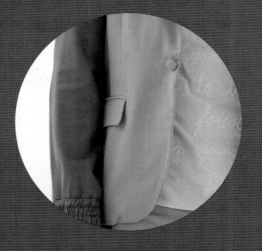

550 SINPATRON
SPAIN

551 EK THONGPRASERT
THAILAND

552 ANA LOCKING
SPAIN

  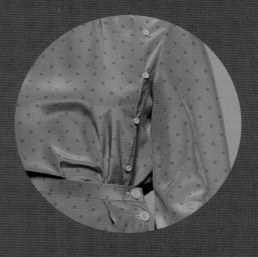

553 AILANTO
SPAIN

554 ELENA PRZHONSKAYA
UKRAINE

555 LEMONIEZ
SPAIN

556 MALAFACHA BRAND
MEXICO

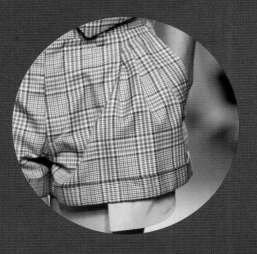

557 ANTONIO ALVARADO
SPAIN

558 ELENA PRZHONSKAYA
UKRAINE

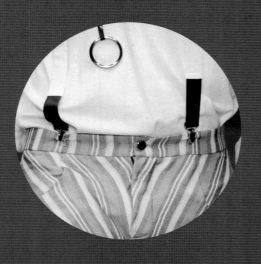

559 HASAN HEJAZI
UK

560 DESIGNSKOLEN
KOLDING
DENMARK

561 LEMONIEZ
SPAIN

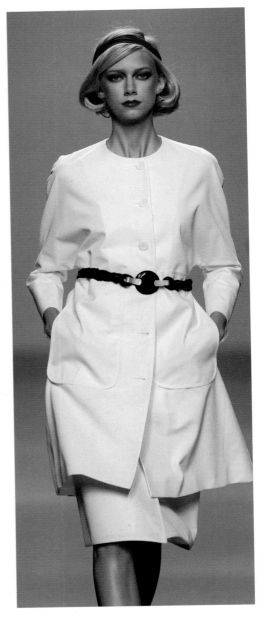

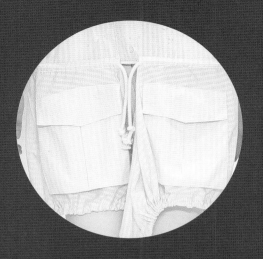

562 RICARDO DOURADO
PORTUGAL

563 EWA I WALLA
SWEDEN

564 KARLOTA LASPALAS
SPAIN

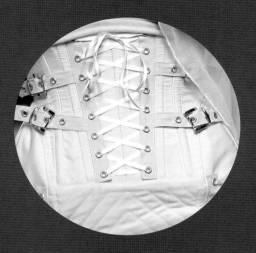

565 RICARDO DOURADO
PORTUGAL

566 BIBIAN BLUE
SPAIN

567 LEMONIEZ
SPAIN

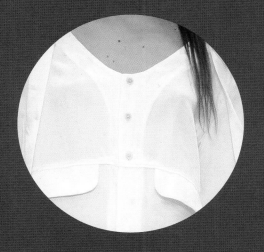

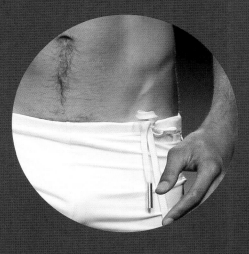

568 RICARDO DOURADO
PORTUGAL

569 ANTONIO ALVARADO
SPAIN

570 MAL-AIMÉE
FRANCE

© Sébastien Agnetti

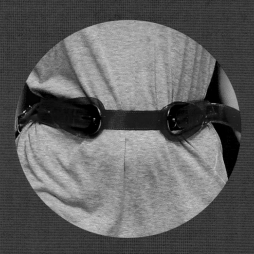

571 NEREA LURGAIN
SPAIN

572 JUANJO OLIVA
SPAIN

573 EK THONGPRASERT
THAILAND

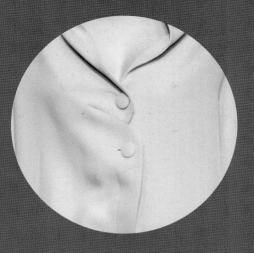

574 JULIUS
JAPAN

575 ALENA AKHMADULLINA
RUSSIA

576 QASIMI
UNITED ARAB EMIRATES

© Étienne Tordoir

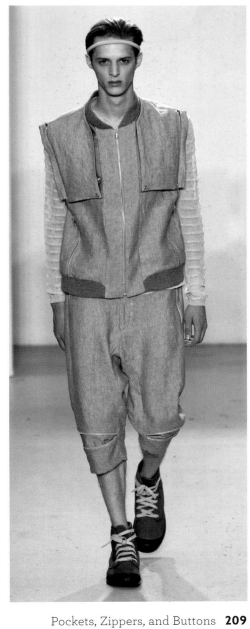

577 KRIS VAN ASSCHE
BELGIUM

578 ION FIZ
SPAIN

579 EWA I WALLA
SWEDEN

© Patrice Stable

© Kristian Löveborg

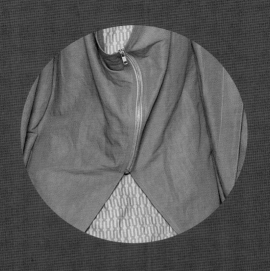

580 QASIMI
UNITED ARAB EMIRATES

581 RICARDO DOURADO
PORTUGAL

582 EWA I WALLA
SWEDEN

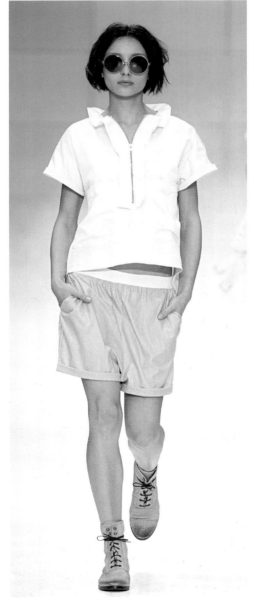

583 OMAR KASHOURA
UK

584 DESIGNSKOLEN
KOLDING
DENMARK

585 DAWID TOMASZEWSKI
POLAND

© Mina Gerngross

586 ASHER LEVINE
USA

587 ELENA SKAKUN
RUSSIA

588 ASHER LEVINE
USA

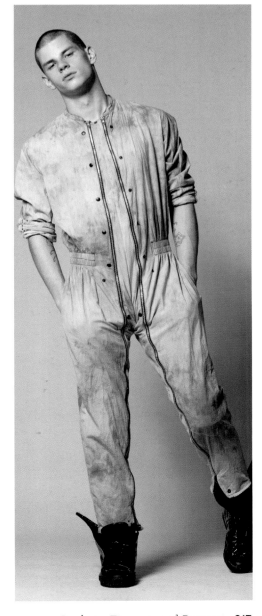

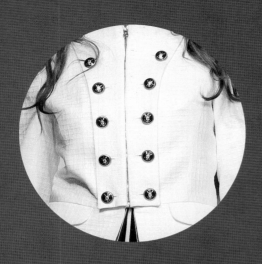

589 STAS LOPATKIN
RUSSIA

590 QASIMI
UNITED ARAB EMIRATES

591 TSUMORI CHISATO
JAPAN

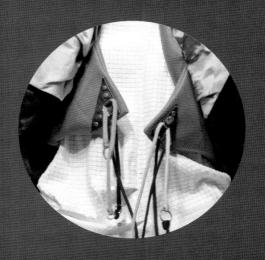

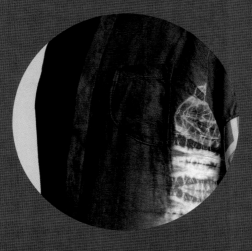

592 SINPATRON
SPAIN

593 ASHER LEVINE
USA

594 DESIGNSKOLEN
KOLDING
DENMARK

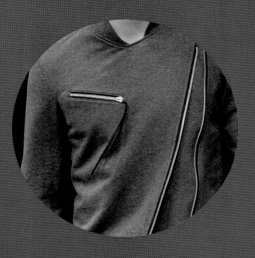

595 ASHER LEVINE
USA

596 JEAN//PHILLIP
DENMARK

597 ASHER LEVINE
USA

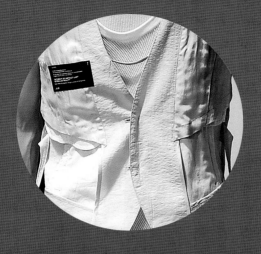

598 JULIUS
JAPAN

599 JEAN//PHILLIP
DENMARK

600 JULIUS
JAPAN

© Étienne Tordoir

© Étienne Tordoir

601 KRIS VAN ASSCHE
BELGIUM

602 EWA I WALLA
SWEDEN

603 QASIMI
UNITED ARAB EMIRATES

© Patrice Stable

© Kristian Löveborg

604 VLADISLAV AKSENOV
RUSSIA

605 DESIGNSKOLEN
KOLDING
DENMARK

606 JEAN//PHILLIP
DENMARK

607 VLADISLAV AKSENOV
RUSSIA

608 SPIJKERS EN SPIJKERS
THE NETHERLANDS

609 ALI CHARISMA
INDONESIA

610 ASGER JUEL LARSEN
DENMARK

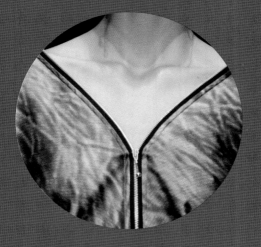

611 DESIGNSKOLEN
KOLDING
DENMARK

612 VLADISLAV AKSENOV
RUSSIA

613 ASHER LEVINE
USA

614 KRIS VAN ASSCHE
BELGIUM

615 CAMILLA NORRBACK
FINLAND

© Patrice Stable

© Kristian Löveborg

616 KARLOTA LASPALAS
SPAIN

617 EWA I WALLA
SWEDEN

618 QASIMI
UNITED ARAB EMIRATES

GATHERING AND DRAPING

Gathering and draping are techniques that give garments an elegant and romantic look, owing to how the fabric hangs and the decorative effects that gathers create. Both are old sewing techniques that date back years and draping, for example, has always been considered a technique linked to haute couture. In current fashion trends, however, both techniques have experienced a resurgence, as this chapter demonstrates. Gathering, a French technique that involves creating fine creases in the fabric, is very much present in sleeves, waistlines, and necklines, creating floral motifs or other embellishments. Draping, which traditionally uses fabrics such as satin, crepe, chiffon, or georgette, now can be achieved with sportier fabrics like cotton and elastane. With some other fabrics, the beauty of the drape and the effect of how the fabric hangs will occur either by purposely adding more material or by stretching on the bias. In this chapter we will study a selection of the simplest gathers and drapes to more elaborate examples of these old sewing techniques.

619 ANJARA
SPAIN

620 BEBA'S CLOSET
SPAIN

621 THE SWEDISH SCHOOL
OF TEXTILES
SWEDEN

© Kristian Löveborg

622 CARLOS DÍEZ
SPAIN

623 LEMONIEZ
SPAIN

624 THE SWEDISH SCHOOL
OF TEXTILES
SWEDEN

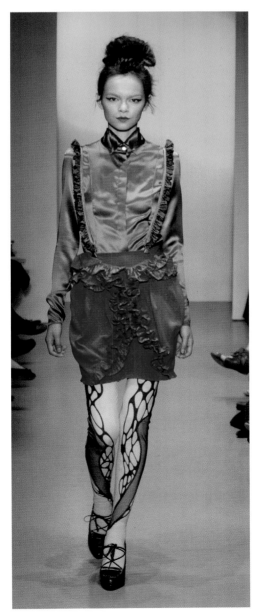

© Kristian Löveborg

Gathering and Draping **227**

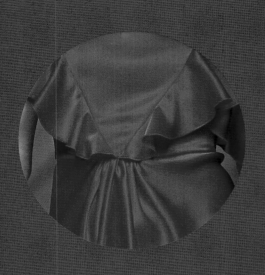

625 BEBA'S CLOSET
SPAIN

626 ANA LOCKING
SPAIN

627 VICTORIO & LUCCHINO
SPAIN

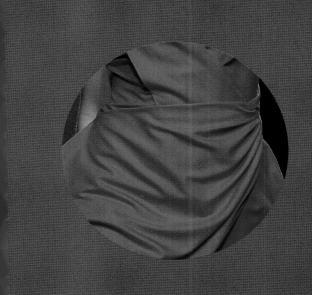

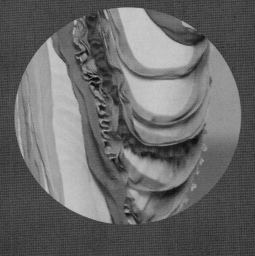

628 JUANJO OLIVA
SPAIN

629 CARLOS DÍEZ
SPAIN

630 VICTORIO & LUCCHINO
SPAIN

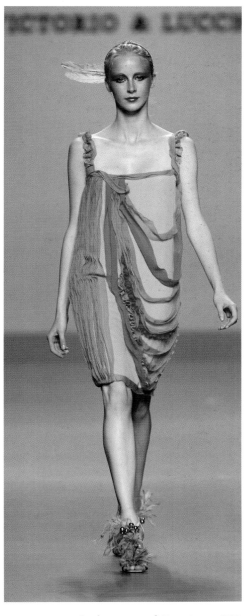

631 THE SWEDISH SCHOOL OF TEXTILES
SWEDEN

632 VICTORIO & LUCCHINO
SPAIN

633 VICTORIO & LUCCHINO
SPAIN

© Kristian Löveborg

634 THE SWEDISH SCHOOL OF TEXTILES
SWEDEN

635 THE SWEDISH SCHOOL OF TEXTILES
SWEDEN

636 VICTORIO & LUCCHINO
SPAIN

© Kristian Löveborg

© Kristian Löveborg

637 MARTIN LAMOTHE
SPAIN

638 ELISA PALOMINO
SPAIN

639 VICTORIO & LUCCHINO
SPAIN

640 AGANOVICH
SERBIA/UK

641 DAWID TOMASZEWSKI
POLAND

642 BEBA'S CLOSET
SPAIN

© Mina Gerngross

643 VICTORIO & LUCCHINO
SPAIN

644 TSUMORI CHISATO
JAPAN

645 ANA LOCKING
SPAIN

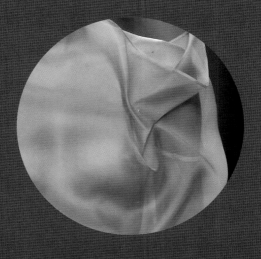

646 DIANA DORADO
COLOMBIA

647 NEREA LURGAIN
SPAIN

648 GEORGIA HARDINGE
UK

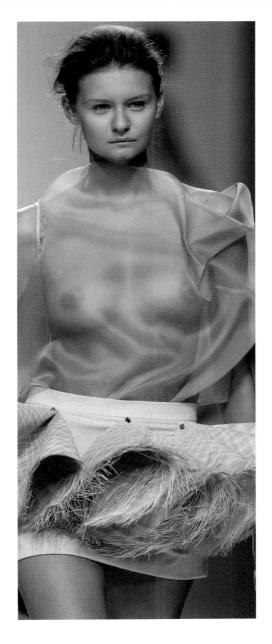

649 ION FIZ
SPAIN

650 VASSILIOS KOSTETSOS
GREECE

651 VICTORIO & LUCCHINO
SPAIN

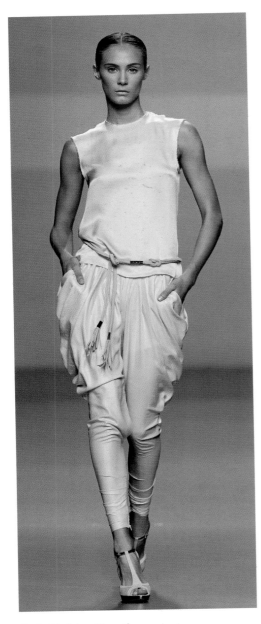

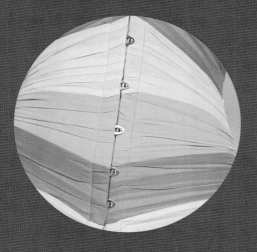

652 TIM VAN STEENBERGEN
BELGIUM

653 VICTORIO & LUCCHINO
SPAIN

654 MAYA HANSEN
SPAIN

655 EWA I WALLA
SWEDEN

656 MALAFACHA BRAND
MEXICO

657 EWA I WALLA
SWEDEN

© Kristian Löveborg

© Kristian Löveborg

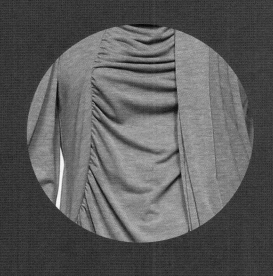

658 ANJARA
SPAIN

659 BOHENTO
SPAIN

660 A.F. VANDEVORST
BELGIUM

661 AILANTO
SPAIN

662 AMERICAN PÉREZ
SPAIN

663 JUANJO OLIVA
SPAIN

664 MARTIN LAMOTHE
SPAIN

665 GEORGIA HARDINGE
UK

666 TSUMORI CHISATO
JAPAN

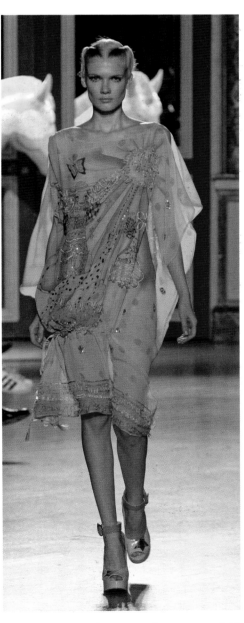

667 MAYA HANSEN
SPAIN

668 JUANJO OLIVA
SPAIN

669 MALAFACHA BRAND
MEXICO

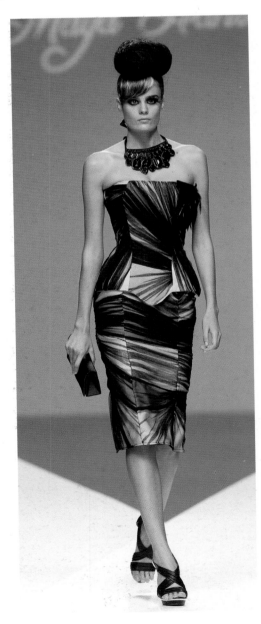

670 EWA I WALLA
SWEDEN

671 ELENA PRZHONSKAYA
UKRAINE

672 BEBA'S CLOSET
SPAIN

© Kristian Löveborg

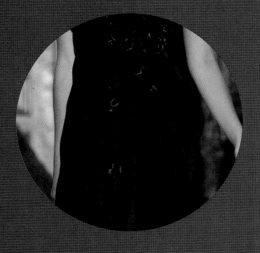

673 KARLOTA LASPALAS
SPAIN

674 RICARDO DOURADO
PORTUGAL

675 HARRIHALIM
INDONESIA

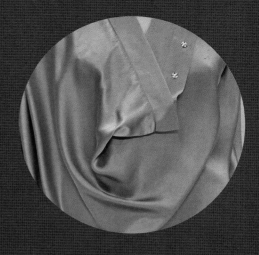

676 RICARDO DOURADO
PORTUGAL

677 DESIGNSKOLEN
KOLDING
DENMARK

678 RICARDO DOURADO
PORTUGAL

679 DIANA DORADO
COLOMBIA

680 TIM VAN STEENBERGEN
BELGIUM

681 JUANJO OLIVA
SPAIN

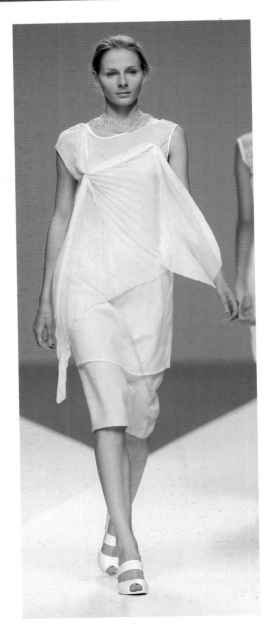

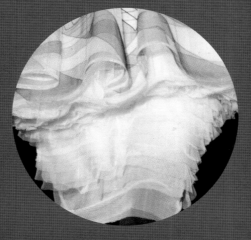

682 GEORGIA HARDINGE
UK

683 ELENA SKAKUN
RUSSIA

684 SINPATRON
SPAIN

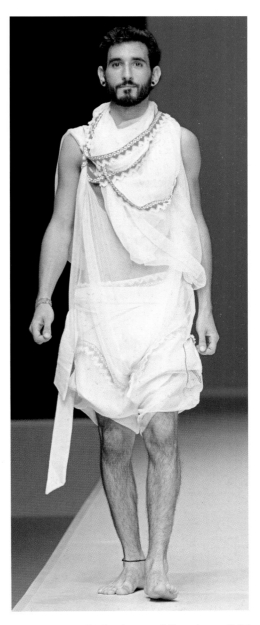

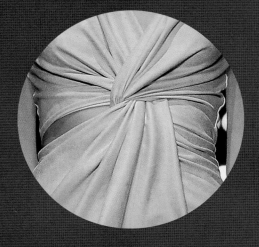

685 BOHENTO
SPAIN

686 DAWID TOMASZEWSKI
POLAND

687 A.F. VANDEVORST
BELGIUM

© Mina Gerngross

688 JEAN//PHILLIP
DENMARK

689 THE SWEDISH SCHOOL
OF TEXTILES
SWEDEN

690 A.F. VANDEVORST
BELGIUM

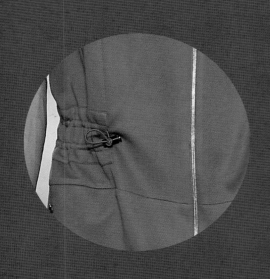

691 QASIMI
UNITED ARAB EMIRATES

692 JUANJO OLIVA
SPAIN

693 JULIUS
JAPAN

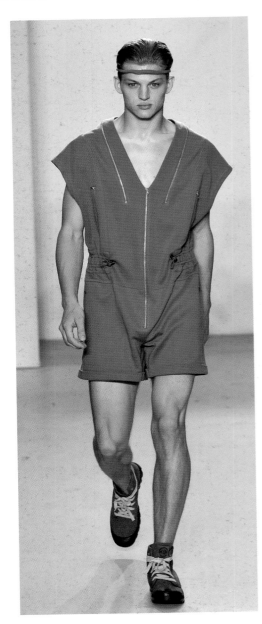

© Étienne Tordoir

694 NEREA LURGAIN
SPAIN

695 EWA I WALLA
SWEDEN

696 ION FIZ
SPAIN

© Kristian Loveborg

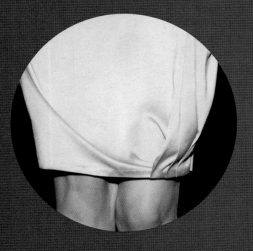

697 ALENA AKHMADULLINA
RUSSIA

698 JEAN//PHILLIP
DENMARK

699 ERICA ZAIONTS
UKRAINE

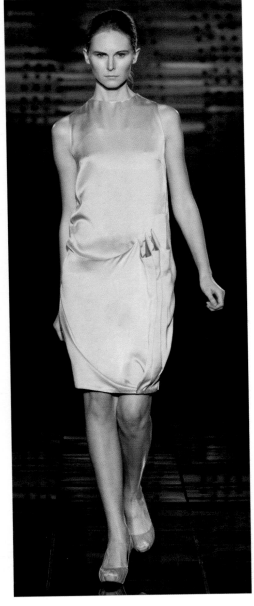

700 THE SWEDISH SCHOOL
OF TEXTILES
SWEDEN

701 ASHER LEVINE
USA

702 THE SWEDISH SCHOOL
OF TEXTILES
SWEDEN

© Kristian Löveborg

© Kristian Löveborg

703 ANJARA
SPAIN

704 TIM VAN STEENBERGEN
BELGIUM

705 ALENA AKHMADULLINA
RUSSIA

© Étienne Tordoir

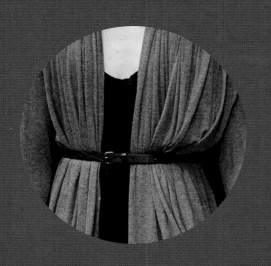

706 JEAN//PHILLIP
DENMARK

707 GEORGIA HARDINGE
UK

708 DESIGNSKOLEN
KOLDING
DENMARK

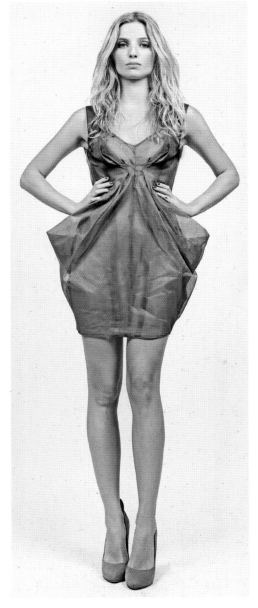

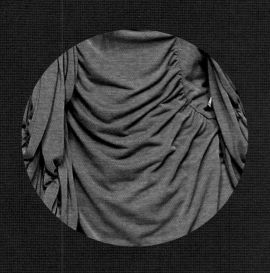

709 ANJARA
SPAIN

710 A.F. VANDEVORST
BELGIUM

711 ALI CHARISMA
INDONESIA

712 BIBIAN BLUE
SPAIN

713 A.F. VANDEVORST
BELGIUM

714 EWA I WALLA
SWEDEN

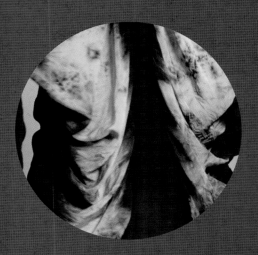

715 **ASHER LEVINE**
USA

716 **TIM VAN STEENBERGEN**
BELGIUM

717 **ANJARA**
SPAIN

© Étienne Tordoir

718 TIM VAN STEENBERGEN
BELGIUM

719 VASSILIOS KOSTETSOS
GREECE

720 TIM VAN STEENBERGEN
BELGIUM

© Étienne Tordoir

© Étienne Tordoir

PLEATS AND FLOUNCES

This chapter showcases the details of the concepts that stand out for their use of timeless and feminine flounces or elegant pleats. Flounces, present on runways around the world year after year, especially in spring and summer, are displayed in dozens of different ways. We will study a selection from small flounces, which add a finishing touch to simple garments, to overelaborate voluminous flounces contributing to a sumptuous, vibrant look. They are perfect to provide volume or flight to skirts, dresses, sleeves, and collars in delicate fabrics such as chiffon, organza, silk, and tulle. Couture designers and experts such as Valentino and Galliano have traditionally drawn inspiration from the influence of Flamenco fashion, which is famous for its feminine flounces. On these pages you will be able to see some of the latest work from the Spanish designers Victorio & Lucchino, the innovative heirs to this art. In addition to the combination of these elements, we will take a look at other techniques, such as pintucks and frills.

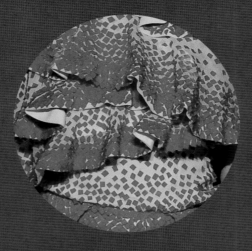
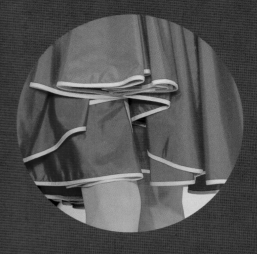

721 DIMITRI
ITALY

722 MANISH ARORA
INDIA

723 MALAFACHA BRAND
MEXICO

© Yannis Vlamos

© Israel Esparza

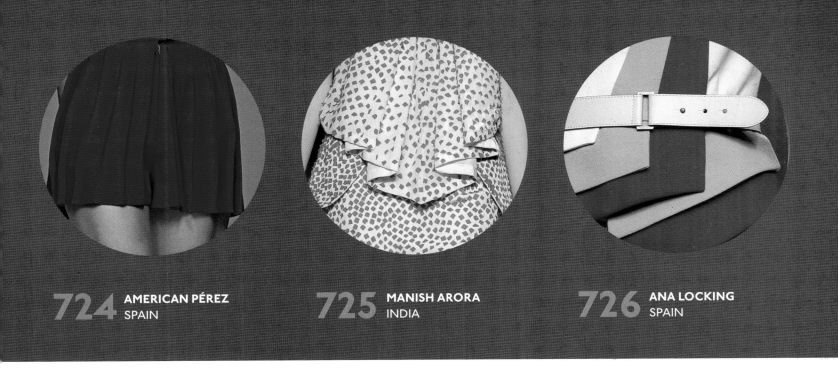

724 AMERICAN PÉREZ
SPAIN

725 MANISH ARORA
INDIA

726 ANA LOCKING
SPAIN

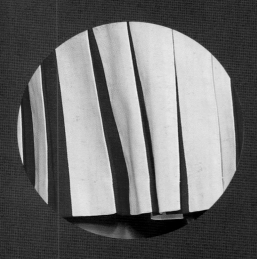
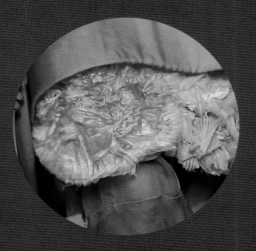

727 AMERICAN PÉREZ
SPAIN

728 VICTORIO & LUCCHINO
SPAIN

729 MALAFACHA BRAND
MEXICO

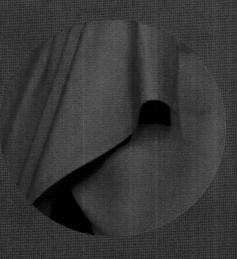

730 MALAFACHA BRAND
MEXICO

731 JUANJO OLIVA
SPAIN

732 BEBA'S CLOSET
SPAIN

© Israel Esparza

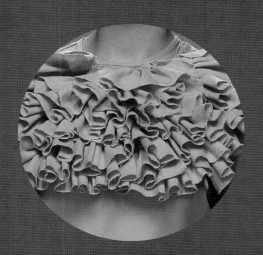

733 DIANA DORADO
COLOMBIA

734 MANISH ARORA
INDIA

735 DIANA DORADO
COLOMBIA

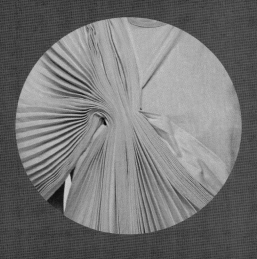

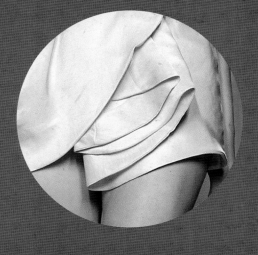

736 IDA SJÖSTEDT
SWEDEN

737 DIANA DORADO
COLOMBIA

738 ION FIZ
SPAIN

© Kristian Löveborg

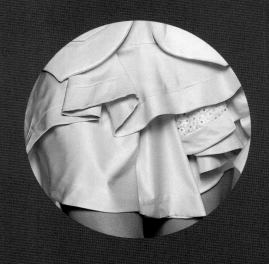

739 AILANTO
SPAIN

740 ELISA PALOMINO
SPAIN

741 ION FIZ
SPAIN

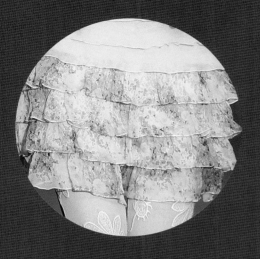

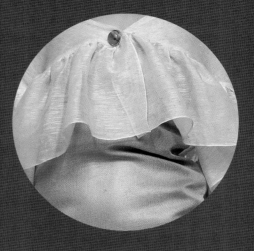

742 ELISA PALOMINO
SPAIN

743 DIANA DORADO
COLOMBIA

744 BEBA'S CLOSET
SPAIN

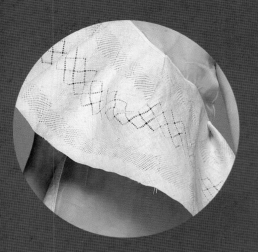

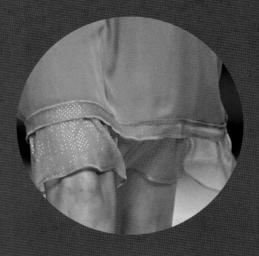

745 DIANA DORADO
COLOMBIA

746 ION FIZ
SPAIN

747 AILANTO
SPAIN

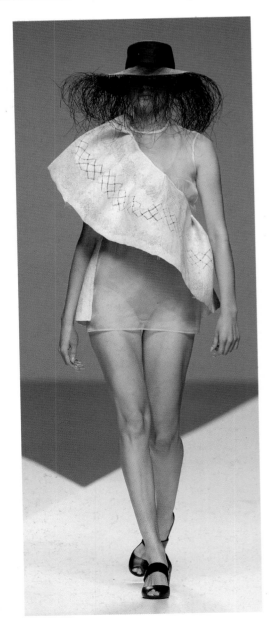

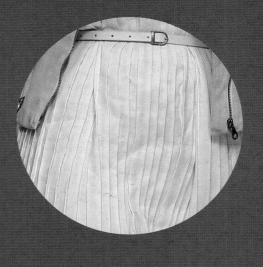

748 ELISA PALOMINO
SPAIN

749 ION FIZ
SPAIN

750 DIANA DORADO
COLOMBIA

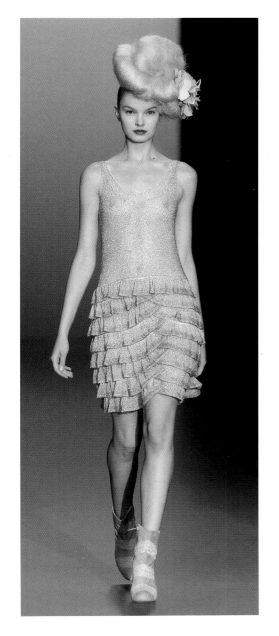

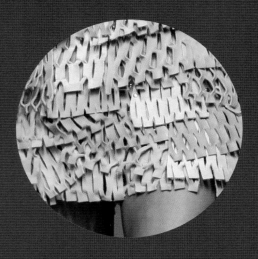

751 EWA I WALLA
SWEDEN

752 G.V.G.V.
JAPAN

753 MARTIN LAMOTHE
SPAIN

© Kristian Löveborg

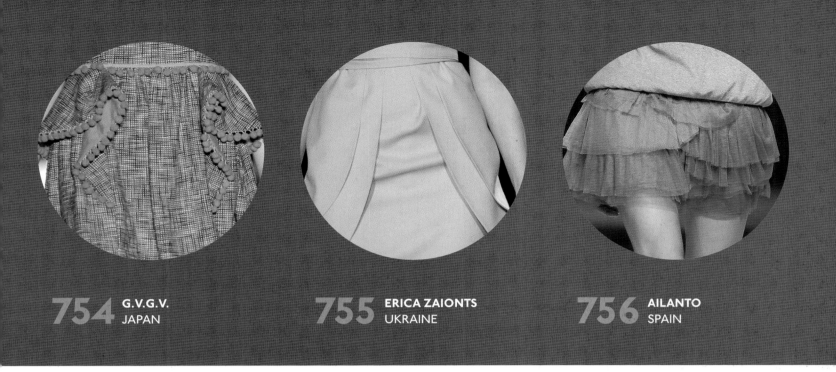

754 G.V.G.V.
JAPAN

755 ERICA ZAIONTS
UKRAINE

756 AILANTO
SPAIN

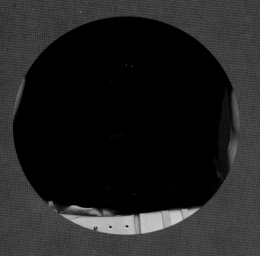

757 TSUMORI CHISATO
JAPAN

758 HARRIHALIM
INDONESIA

759 ANA LOCKING
SPAIN

760 IDA SJÖSTEDT
SWEDEN

761 MALAFACHA BRAND
MEXICO

762 CARLOS DÍEZ
SPAIN

© Kristian Löveborg

© Israel Esparza

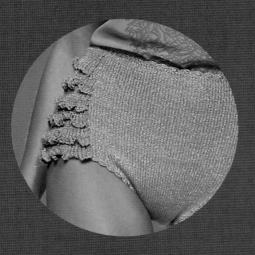

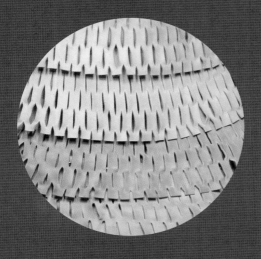

763 MANISH ARORA
INDIA

764 CATI SERRÀ
SPAIN

765 MARTIN LAMOTHE
SPAIN

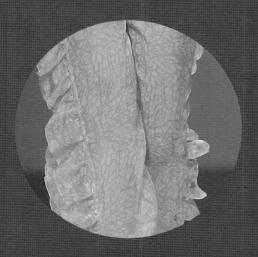

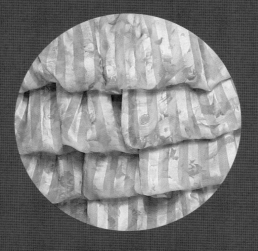

766 CATI SERRÀ
SPAIN

767 DIANA DORADO
COLOMBIA

768 ELENA PRZHONSKAYA
UKRAINE

769 ELISA PALOMINO
SPAIN

770 DIANA DORADO
COLOMBIA

771 IDA SJÖSTEDT
SWEDEN

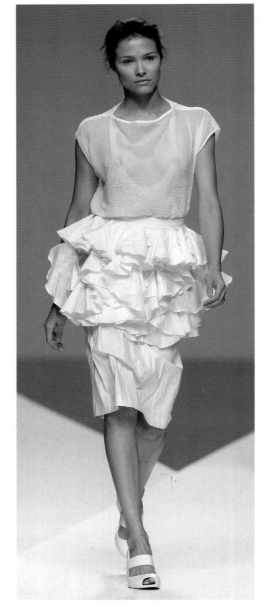

© Kristian Löveborg

772 EWA I WALLA
SWEDEN

773 CATI SERRÀ
SPAIN

774 IDA SJÖSTEDT
SWEDEN

© Kristian Löveborg

© Kristian Löveborg

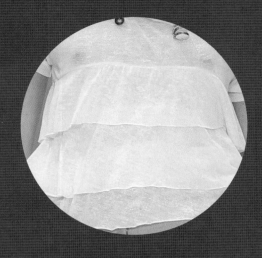

775 DIANA DORADO
COLOMBIA

776 IDA SJÖSTEDT
SWEDEN

777 RICARDO DOURADO
PORTUGAL

© Kristian Löveborg

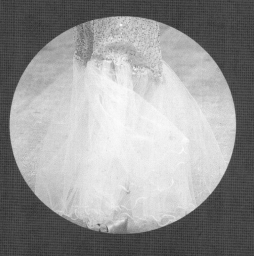

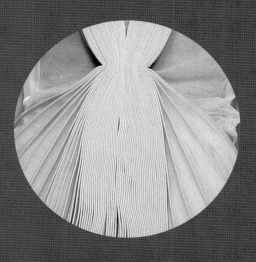

778 DIANA DORADO
COLOMBIA

779 IDA SJÖSTEDT
SWEDEN

780 DIANA DORADO
COLOMBIA

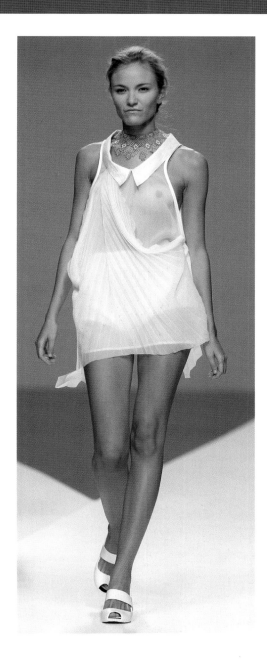

© Kristian Löveborg

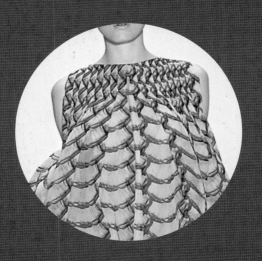

781 DAWID TOMASZEWSKI
POLAND

782 CAMILLA NORRBACK
FINLAND

783 EWA I WALLA
SWEDEN

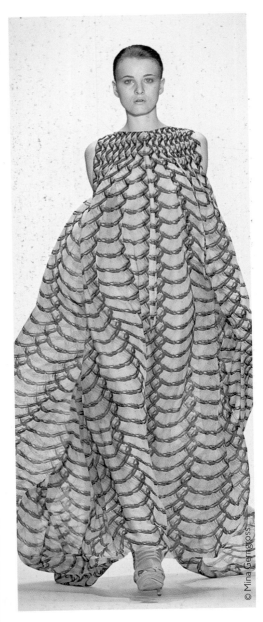
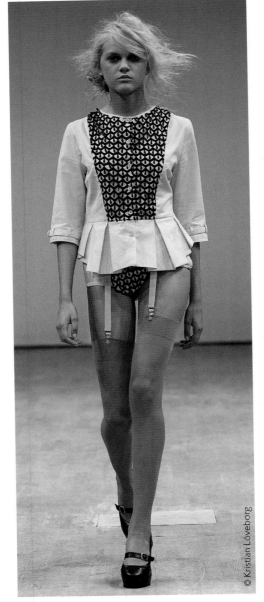

784 VASSILIOS KOSTETSOS
GREECE

785 DAWID TOMASZEWSKI
POLAND

786 MALAFACHA BRAND
MEXICO

© Mina Gerngross

Pleats and Flounces **283**

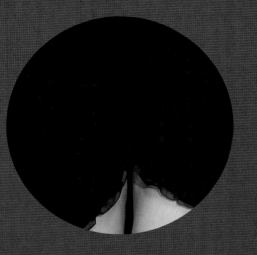

787 DAWID TOMASZEWSKI
POLAND

788 ELISA PALOMINO
SPAIN

789 GEORGIA HARDINGE
UK

© Mina Gerngross

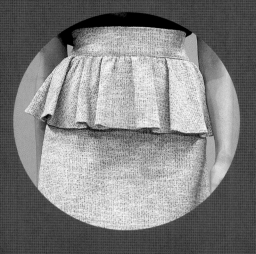

790 ERICA ZAIONTS
UKRAINE

791 CAMILLA NORRBACK
FINLAND

792 BORA AKSU
TURKEY

© Kristian Löveborg

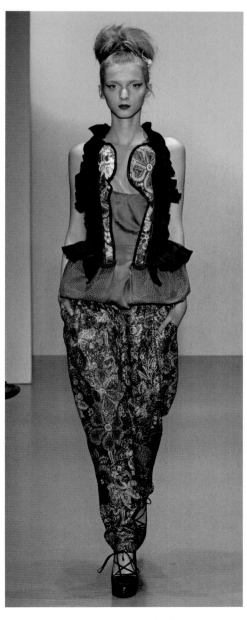

793 TSUMORI CHISATO
JAPAN

794 ELISA PALOMINO
SPAIN

795 HARRIHALIM
INDONESIA

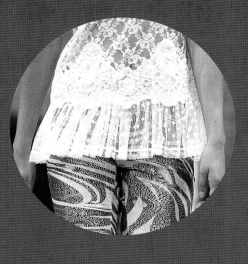

796 TSUMORI CHISATO
JAPAN

797 IDA SJÖSTEDT
SWEDEN

798 EWA I WALLA
SWEDEN

© Kristian Löveborg

© Kristian Löveborg

DECORATIVE APPLIQUÉS

Decorative appliqués offer a wide range of possibilities. By adding the perfect piece, many designers covert a garment into a must-have of the season. International runways are brimming with studs, sequins, feathers, rhinestones, beads, ribbons, strings, fringes, tassels, braids, paintings, and many more accessories in this fantasy world. In this chapter we will see elements like military-inspired epaulettes, satin ribbons and Baroque-style beaded corsets, or fragile items such as Swarovski crystals, which can be seen in the Canadian designer Mark Fast's latest collection, featured at London Fashion Week. Trends revive elements such as feathers and beading and new concepts, like long artificial hair, vinyl applications, wires, and craftwork, such as painting done by hand, and other decorative motifs, complement the latest fashions. Tradition and ethnic resources are also a recurring feature in these designs.

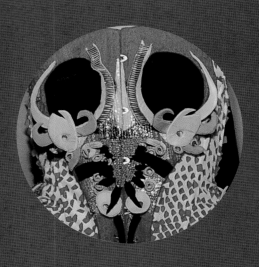

799 MANISH ARORA
INDIA

800 MALINI RAMANI
USA/INDIA

801 MALAFACHA BRAND
MEXICO

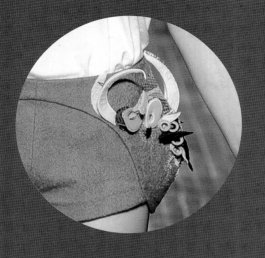

802 MALINI RAMANI
USA/INDIA

803 MANISH ARORA
INDIA

804 AMERICAN PÉREZ
SPAIN

805 TSUMORI CHISATO
JAPAN

806 MALAFACHA BRAND
MEXICO

807 MARK FAST
CANADA

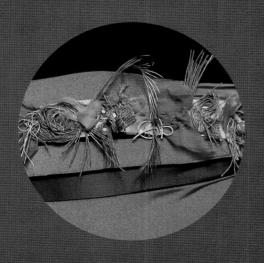

808 VICTORIO & LUCCHINO
SPAIN

809 AMERICAN PÉREZ
SPAIN

810 MALAFACHA BRAND
MEXICO

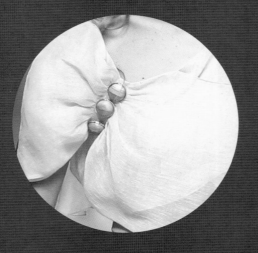

811 **MARCEL OSTERTAG**
GERMANY

812 **BEBA'S CLOSET**
SPAIN

813 **VICTORIO & LUCCHINO**
SPAIN

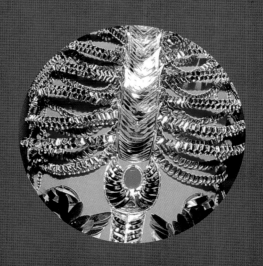

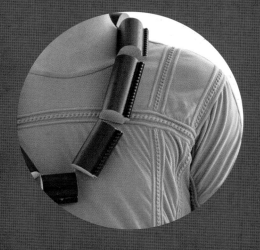

814 MANISH ARORA
INDIA

815 G.V.G.V.
JAPAN

816 EK THONGPRASERT
THAILAND

© Yannis Vlamos

Decorative Appliqués **295**

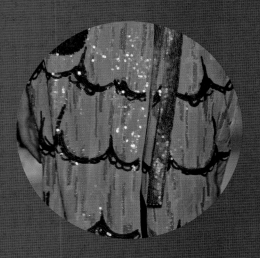

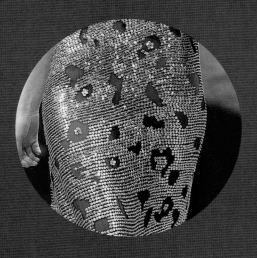

817 **TSUMORI CHISATO**
JAPAN

818 **IDA SJÖSTEDT**
SWEDEN

819 **SINPATRON**
SPAIN

© Kristian Loveborg

820 **DESIGNSKOLEN KOLDING**
DENMARK

821 **MALAFACHA BRAND**
MEXICO

822 **TSUMORI CHISATO**
JAPAN

© Israel Esparza

823 ANJARA
SPAIN

824 DESIGNSKOLEN
KOLDING
DENMARK

825 BIBIAN BLUE
SPAIN

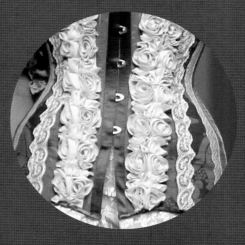

826 G.V.G.V.
JAPAN

827 BIBIAN BLUE
SPAIN

828 ANTONIO ALVARADO
SPAIN

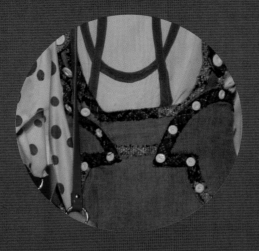

829 **MALAFACHA BRAND**
MEXICO

830 **TSUMORI CHISATO**
JAPAN

831 **EK THONGPRASERT**
THAILAND

832 BIBIAN BLUE
SPAIN

833 TSUMORI CHISATO
JAPAN

834 MALAFACHA BRAND
MEXICO

© Israel Esparza

Decorative Appliqués **301**

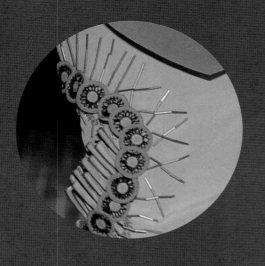

835 MANISH ARORA
INDIA

836 BEBA'S CLOSET
SPAIN

837 MANISH ARORA
INDIA

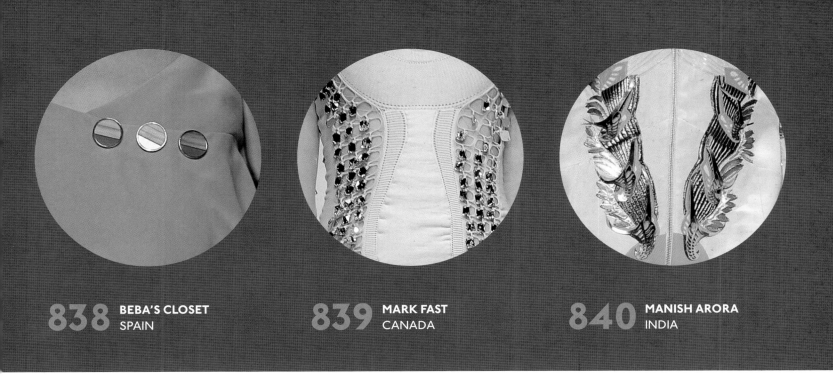

838 BEBA'S CLOSET
SPAIN

839 MARK FAST
CANADA

840 MANISH ARORA
INDIA

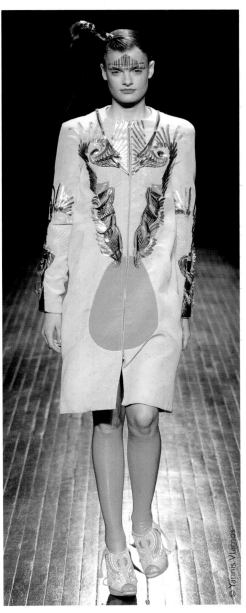

841 AILANTO
SPAIN

842 MALAFACHA BRAND
MEXICO

843 VICTORIO & LUCCHINO
SPAIN

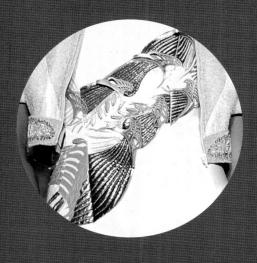

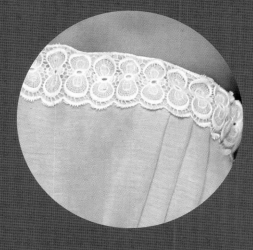

844 MANISH ARORA
INDIA

845 DIANA DORADO
COLOMBIA

846 BEBA'S CLOSET
SPAIN

© Yannis Vlamos

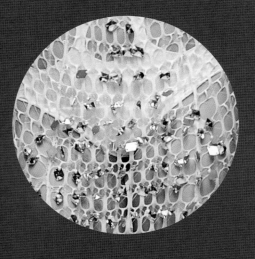

847 MANISH ARORA
INDIA

848 ION FIZ
SPAIN

249 MARK FAST
CANADA

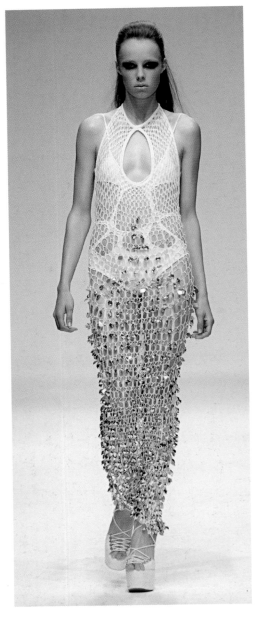

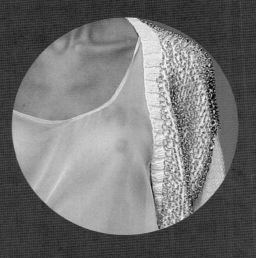

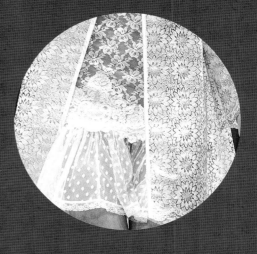

850 **STAS LOPATKIN**
RUSSIA

851 **CATI SERRÀ**
SPAIN

852 **IDA SJÖSTEDT**
SWEDEN

© Kristian Löveborg

853 MAYA HANSEN
SPAIN

854 TSUMORI CHISATO
JAPAN

855 AMERICAN PÉREZ
SPAIN

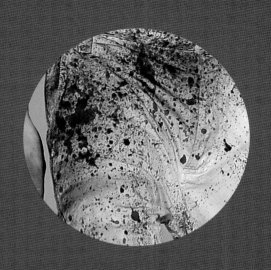

856 KRIS VAN ASSCHE
BELGIUM

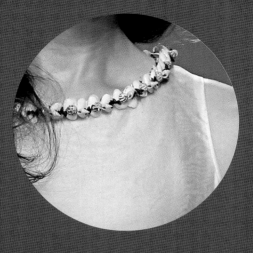

857 AMERICAN PÉREZ
SPAIN

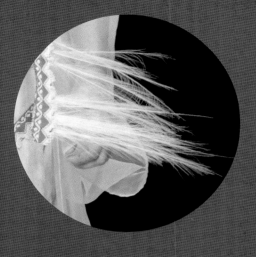

858 SINPATRON
SPAIN

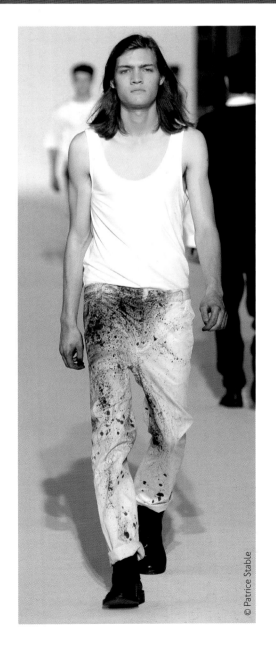

© Patrice Stable

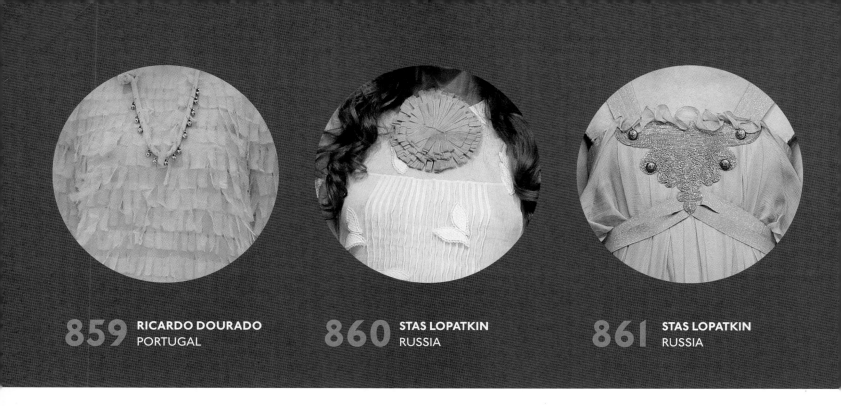

859 RICARDO DOURADO
PORTUGAL

860 STAS LOPATKIN
RUSSIA

861 STAS LOPATKIN
RUSSIA

862 ELISA PALOMINO
SPAIN

863 VASSILIOS KOSTETSOS
GREECE

864 EK THONGPRASERT
THAILAND

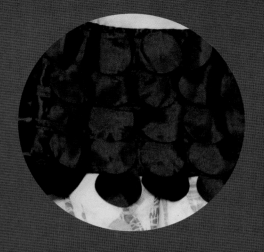

865 GEORGIA HARDINGE
UK

866 ALI CHARISMA
INDONESIA

867 DESIGNSKOLEN KOLDING
DENMARK

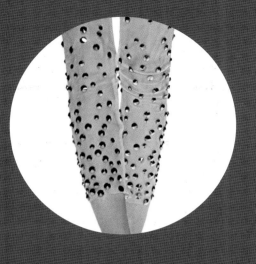

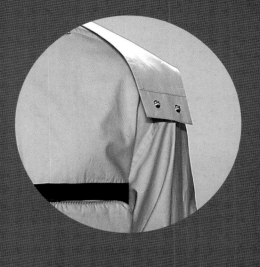

868 ALI CHARISMA
INDONESIA

869 DAWID TOMASZEWSKI
POLAND

870 QASIMI
UNITED ARAB EMIRATES

Decorative Appliqués **313**

871 RICARDO DOURADO
PORTUGAL

872 ELISA PALOMINO
SPAIN

873 VLADISLAV AKSENOV
RUSSIA

874 ELISA PALOMINO
SPAIN

875 VLADISLAV AKSENOV
RUSSIA

876 VASSILIOS KOSTETSOS
GREECE

877 MAYA HANSEN
SPAIN

878 MAL-AIMÉE
FRANCE

879 HARRIHALIM
INDONESIA

© Sébastien Agnetti

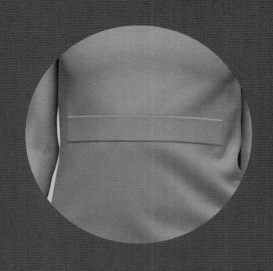

880 J JS LEE
KOREA

881 TIM VAN STEENBERGEN
BELGIUM

882 BIBIAN BLUE
SPAIN

883 ELISA PALOMINO
SPAIN

884 MARK FAST
CANADA

885 TSUMORI CHISATO
JAPAN

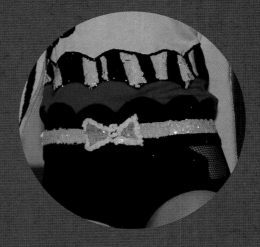

886 HARRIHALIM
INDONESIA

887 ELISA PALOMINO
SPAIN

888 TSUMORI CHISATO
JAPAN

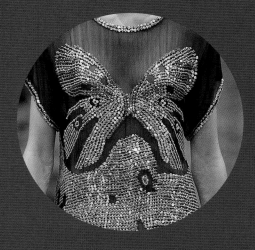

889 **DESIGNSKOLEN KOLDING** DENMARK

890 **DIMITRI** ITALY

891 **IDA SJÖSTEDT** SWEDEN

892 ALI CHARISMA
INDONESIA

893 AMERICAN PÉREZ
SPAIN

894 DIMITRI
ITALY

895 ASHER LEVINE
USA

896 BIBIAN BLUE
SPAIN

897 ELISA PALOMINO
SPAIN

898 ASGER JUEL LARSEN
DENMARK

899 HARRIHALIM
INDONESIA

900 MARTIN LAMOTHE
SPAIN

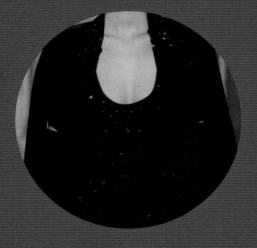

901 ASHER LEVINE
USA

902 HARRIHALIM
INDONESIA

903 MAYA HANSEN
SPAIN

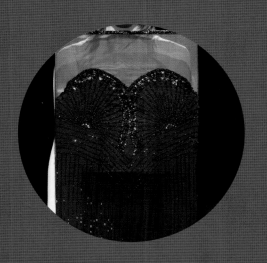

904 ELENA PRZHONSKAYA
UKRAINE

905 ASGER JUEL LARSEN
DENMARK

906 MAYA HANSEN
SPAIN

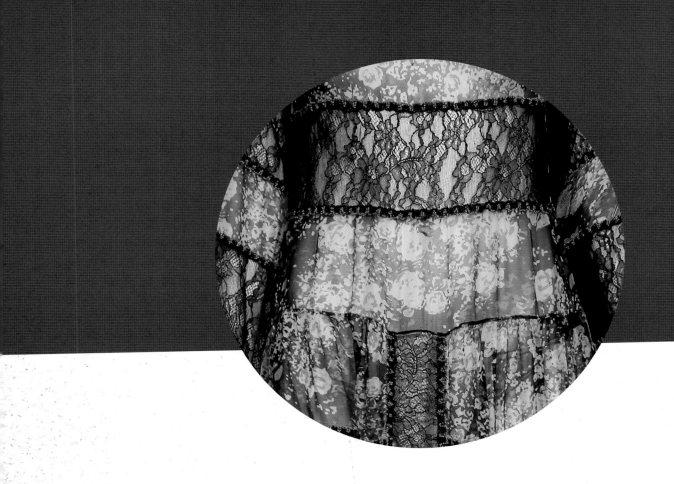

SEWING DETAILS

In this last chapter we will focus on the sewing details that at times are less visible but no less important or significant when appreciating a garment. On the one hand, we will study pure sewing elements such as bust and hip darts and French seams, used in transparent garments, etc. This chapter includes all those elements that have traditionally been used to sculpt the silhouette and add the finishing touches to garments and now play an important role in the deconstructed garment, in volumes, architectural forms, and asymmetries that are such a prominent feature in modern design. Lace edging, blond lace, or yokes complete this section along with different styles of embroidery, depending on the type of knot used in the work. This chapter also highlights the appliqué work, which is embroidered separately and then superimposed on the garment. It represents a fusion of details from the finest ateliers and the hardest working hands.

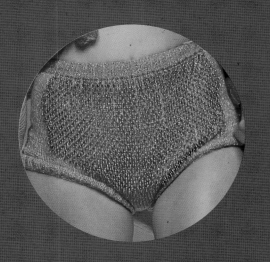

907 CATI SERRÀ
SPAIN

908 THE SWEDISH SCHOOL
OF TEXTILES
SWEDEN

909 ELISA PALOMINO
SPAIN

© Kristian Löveborg

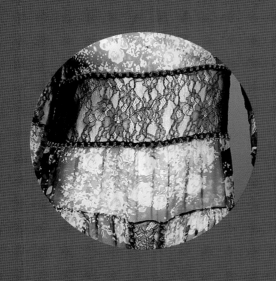

910 ELISA PALOMINO
SPAIN

911 THE SWEDISH SCHOOL
OF TEXTILES
SWEDEN

912 ELISA PALOMINO
SPAIN

© Kristian Löveborg

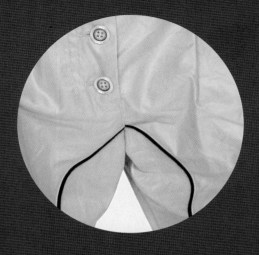

913 ANA LOCKING
SPAIN

914 ELISA PALOMINO
SPAIN

915 MARCEL OSTERTAG
GERMANY

916 AILANTO
SPAIN

917 DESIGNSKOLEN
KOLDING
DENMARK

918 MAYA HANSEN
SPAIN

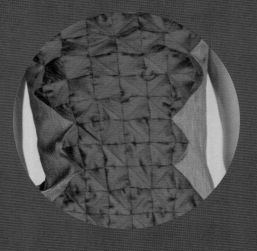

919 VASSILIOS KOSTETSOS
GREECE

920 ADA ZANDITON
UK

921 MARTIN LAMOTHE
SPAIN

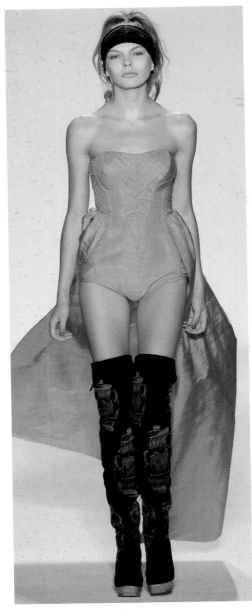

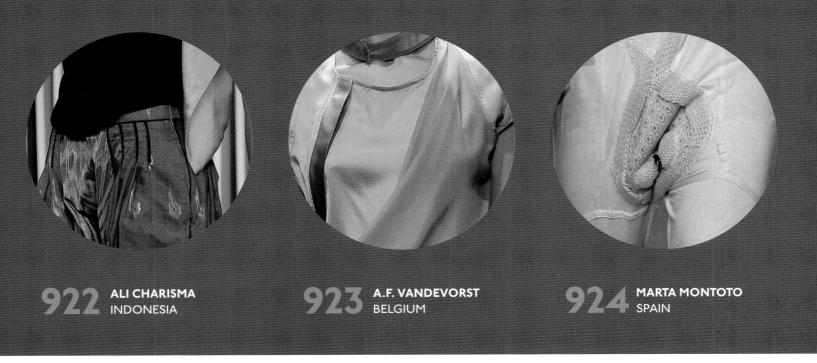

922 ALI CHARISMA
INDONESIA

923 A.F. VANDEVORST
BELGIUM

924 MARTA MONTOTO
SPAIN

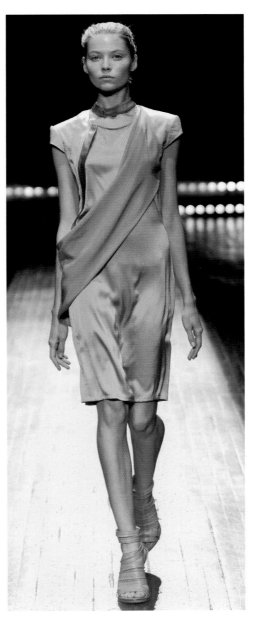

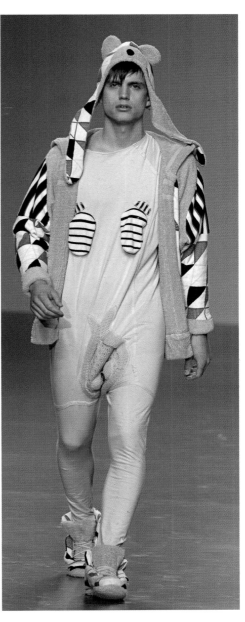

925 KARLOTA LASPALAS
SPAIN

926 AILANTO
SPAIN

927 A.F. VANDEVORST
BELGIUM

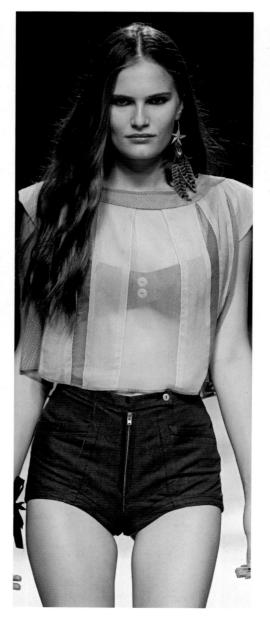

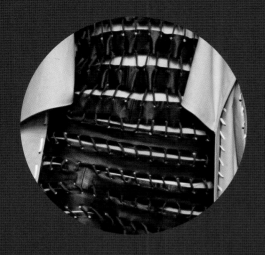

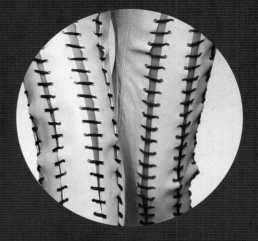

928 MARTIN LAMOTHE
SPAIN

929 ELENA PRZHONSKAYA
UKRAINE

930 MARTIN LAMOTHE
SPAIN

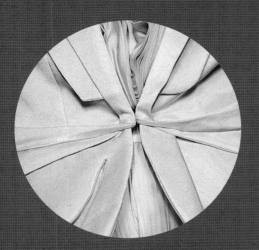

931 **ION FIZ**
SPAIN

932 **DESIGNSKOLEN KOLDING**
DENMARK

933 **BOHENTO**
SPAIN

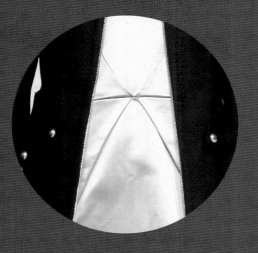

934 A.F. VANDEVORST
BELGIUM

935 STAS LOPATKIN
RUSSIA

936 THE SWEDISH SCHOOL OF TEXTILES
SWEDEN

© Kristian Löveborg

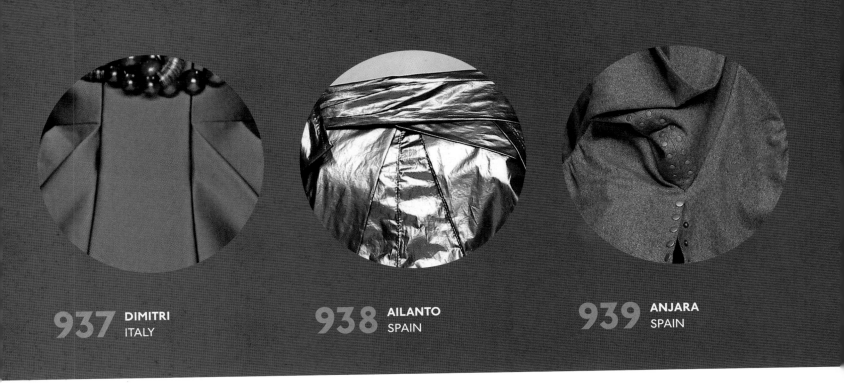

937 DIMITRI
ITALY

938 AILANTO
SPAIN

939 ANJARA
SPAIN

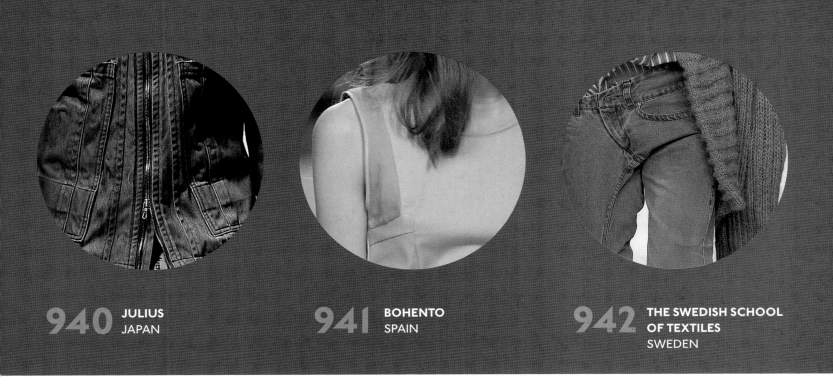

940 JULIUS
JAPAN

941 BOHENTO
SPAIN

942 THE SWEDISH SCHOOL
OF TEXTILES
SWEDEN

© Étienne Tordoir

© Kristian Löveborg

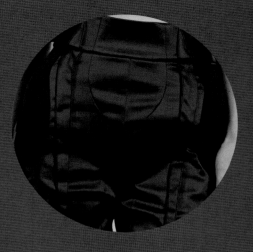

943 ERICA ZAIONTS
UKRAINE

944 MAL-AIMÉE
FRANCE

945 DESIGNSKOLEN
KOLDING
DENMARK

© Sébastien Agnetti

946 **DESIGNSKOLEN KOLDING**
DENMARK

947 **HARRIHALIM**
INDONESIA

948 **VASSILIOS KOSTETSOS**
GREECE

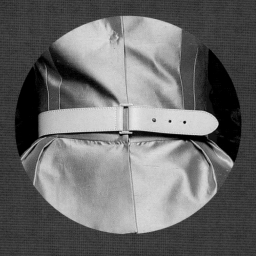

949 MANISH ARORA
INDIA

950 ADA ZANDITON
UK

951 ANA LOCKING
SPAIN

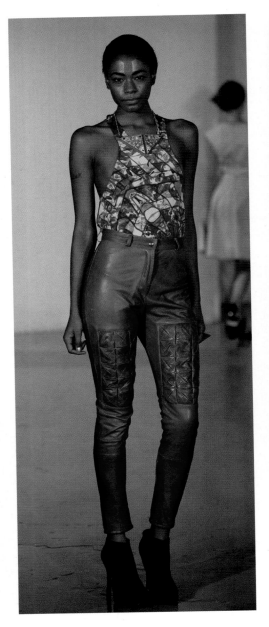

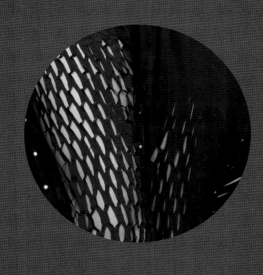

952 MARTIN LAMOTHE
SPAIN

953 CRAIG LAWRENCE
UK

954 ION FIZ
SPAIN

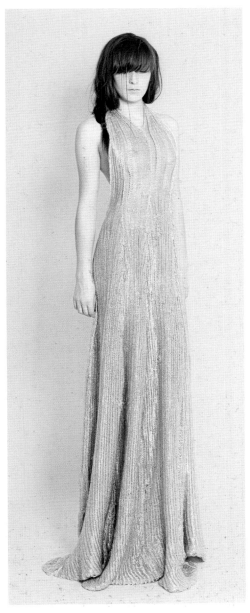

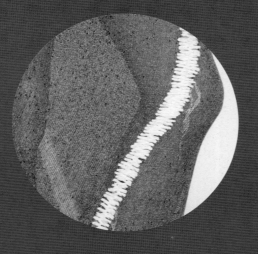

955 ADA ZANDITON
UK

956 CRAIG LAWRENCE
UK

957 ANA LOCKING
SPAIN

958 CRAIG LAWRENCE
UK

959 BEBA'S CLOSET
SPAIN

960 CRAIG LAWRENCE
UK

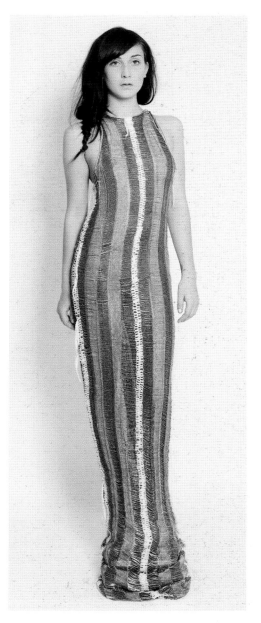

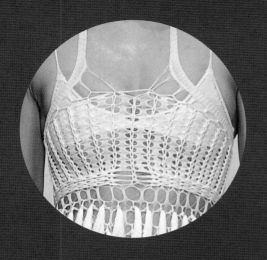

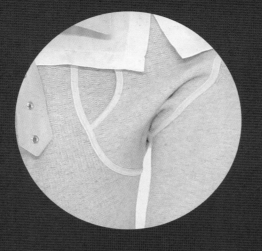

961 MARK FAST
CANADA

962 RICARDO DOURADO
PORTUGAL

963 CRAIG LAWRENCE
UK

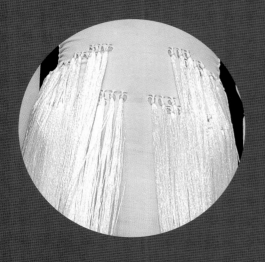

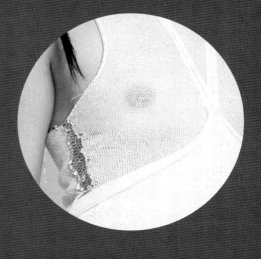

964 MARK FAST
CANADA

965 IDA SJÖSTEDT
SWEDEN

966 CRAIG LAWRENCE
UK

© Kristian Löveborg

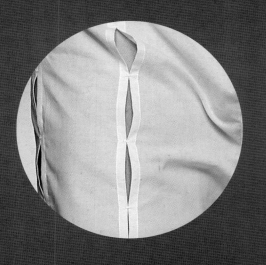

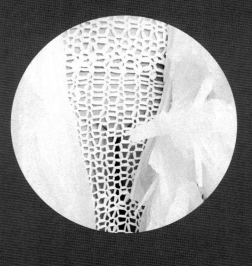

967 CARLOS DÍEZ
SPAIN

968 CRAIG LAWRENCE
UK

969 ION FIZ
SPAIN

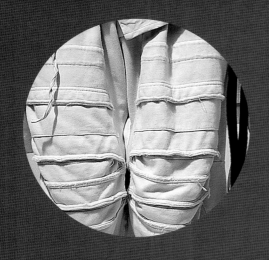

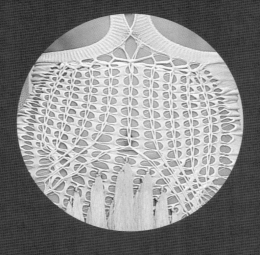

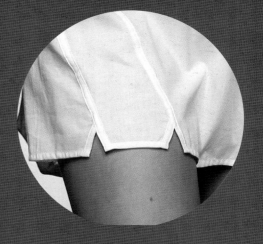

970 JULIUS
JAPAN

971 MARK FAST
CANADA

972 CARLOS DÍEZ
SPAIN

© Étienne Tordoir

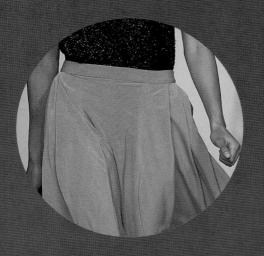

973 DESIGNSKOLEN
KOLDING
DENMARK

974 ELISA PALOMINO
SPAIN

975 THE SWEDISH SCHOOL
OF TEXTILES
SWEDEN

© Kristian Löveborg

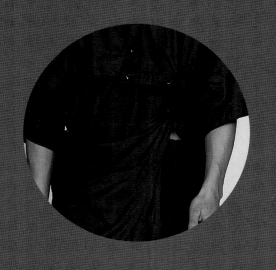

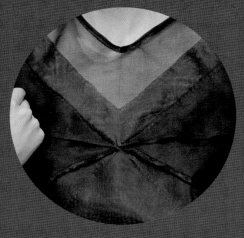

976 THE SWEDISH SCHOOL OF TEXTILES
SWEDEN

977 DESIGNSKOLEN KOLDING
DENMARK

978 CAMILLA NORRBACK
FINLAND

© Kristian Löveborg

© Kristian Löveborg

979 QASIMI
UNITED ARAB EMIRATES

980 ELENA SKAKUN
RUSSIA

981 VLADISLAV AKSENOV
RUSSIA

982 ALI CHARISMA
INDONESIA

983 VLADISLAV AKSENOV
RUSSIA

984 SPIJKERS EN SPIJKERS
THE NETHERLANDS

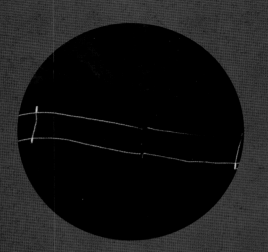

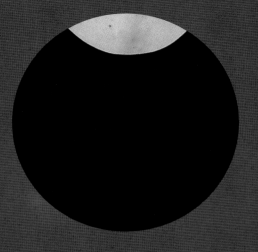

985 KRIS VAN ASSCHE
BELGIUM

986 GEORGIA HARDINGE
UK

987 KRIS VAN ASSCHE
BELGIUM

© Patrice Stable

© Patrice Stable

988 MARK FAST
CANADA

989 VLADISLAV AKSENOV
RUSSIA

990 SPIJKERS EN SPIJKERS
THE NETHERLANDS

991 DESIGNSKOLEN KOLDING
DENMARK

992 KRIS VAN ASSCHE
BELGIUM

993 GEORGIA HARDINGE
UK

© Patrice Stable

994 JULIUS
JAPAN

995 DESIGNSKOLEN
KOLDING
DENMARK

996 HARRIHALIM
INDONESIA

© Étienne Tordoir

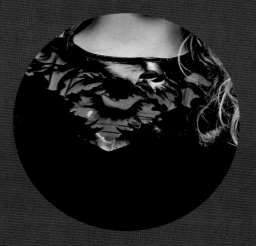

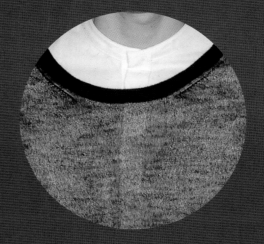

997 JULIUS
JAPAN

998 GEORGIA HARDINGE
UK

999 KRIS VAN ASSCHE
BELGIUM

© Étienne Tordoir

© Patrice Stable

A.F. VANDEVORST
www.afvandevorst.be

An Vandevorst and Filip Arickx, A.F. Vandevorst, met in 1987 while studying at the Royal Academy of Fine Arts in Antwerp, Belgium. Later, An worked as chief assistant for Dries Van Noten and Filip worked as a freelance designer for fashion houses and as a stylist. In 1998, they joined forces to create a womenswear label, and since then they have presented their expressive collections bursting with personality in the Paris Fashion Week. They won the Venus Fashion Award for their debut on this runway.

ADA ZANDITON
www.adaz.co.uk

Ada Zanditon is a London-based designer who studied at the London College of Fashion, specializing in women's clothing. Throughout her career, she has worked in fashion houses such as Alexander McQueen, Jonathan Saunders, and Gareth Pugh. She created her own company in 2008 with a distinctive ethnic flavor, and made her official runway debut at London Fashion Week, where she received rave reviews. She has also created costumes for musicians such as Patrick Wolf and celebrities such as Dita Von Teese and Lois Winstone.

AGANOVICH
www.aganovich.com

Aganovich is the womenswear clothing label based in London designed by Nana Aganovich with narrative and conceptual influences devised by Brooke Taylor. Nana is a graduate of Dansk Designskole, with a masters from Central Saint Martins. Taylor is a former essayist and contributor for international literary and fashion magazines. After having presented collections at London Fashion Week, Aganovich has shown at Paris Fashion Week since 2009.

AILANTO
www.ailanto.com

Ailanto is the label created by the twin bothers Iñaki and Aitor Muñoz. Born in Bilbao, Spain in 1968, the designers moved to Barcelona where they graduated in fine arts at the University of Barcelona UB. Iñaki complemented his studies with a degree in fashion design. The label's elegant collections are renowned for their geometric forms and artistic or cinematographic references. The collections have been sold internationally since 1995 with acclaimed runway presentations in Cibeles Madrid Fashion Week since 2001.

ALENA AKHMADULLINA
www.alenaakhmadullina.com

The Russian designer Alena Akhmadullina is a Saint Petersburg Technology and Design Academy graduate. She presented her first prêt-à-porter collection at Paris Fashion Week in 2005 and since then she has presented a new collection on the French runway each season. In 2007, Alena opened an office in Moscow and opened her first store in the center of the city the following year. Alena Akhmadullina collections constitute a unique universe that combines Russian audacity with a Parisian sense of style.

ALI CHARISMA
www.alicharisma.com

Ali Charisma's label began more than seven years ago, when he opened his first store in Seminyak, Indonesia. His design is characterized by the extreme opposition of color and texture. After achieving a balance between business and creativity, he began to show collections at fashion weeks in Bali, Jakarta, Hong Kong, and Kuala Lumpur. His position in Bali as the president of the Indonesian Fashion Designers Association allows him to actively participate in developing fashion design in his country.

AMERICAN PÉREZ
www.americanperez.es

American Pérez is the brainchild of Natalia Pérez and Jorge Bolado Moo. Natalia is a graduate of the ESDi School of Design in Barcelona and the University of Southampton; Jorge has a degree in fine arts from the University of Vigo and went on to receive a master's degree in styling from the Escola BAU in Barcelona, Spain. Together they created American Pérez in 2008, and have presented collections in Createurope Berlin and in El Ego de Cibeles, where they won the L'Oréal prize for the best fall/winter 2011 collection. They have also been finalists for the ModaFAD awards.

ANA LOCKING
www.analocking.com

Ana González created Locking Shocking in 1996. For ten years, before the dissolution of the company, she received awards as the Prix de la moda Marie Claire for the best national designer in 2004. She founded her new label Ana Locking in 2008. Her debut collection won the L'Oréal Paris Award for the best collection from Cibeles Madrid Fashion Week. In 2009, she presented her collection in the New York Public Library during New York Fashion Week and won the Cosmopolitan Award for the best designer of the year.

ANJARA
www.anjara.com

Anjara García was born in Seville, Spain, and now resides in Shanghai, China where she combines her role as a designer with her role as a DJ playing music in the best clubs. She studied Fashion Design at the Llotja School of Art and Design in Barcelona, Spain. In 2003, she opened her showroom in Seville, Spain and has since presented collection on runways such as Atmosphère in Paris, SIMM in Madrid, and in shows such as Bread & Butter Berlin and Who's Next in Paris. In 2006, she opened her own store in Madrid and we can now see her designs at Cibeles Madrid Fashion Week.

ANNA MIMINOSHVILI
www.a-nic-o.com

The Russian designer Anna Miminoshvili inherited her talent from her architect parents. In her collections, she expresses her taste through architectural forms and elegant lines. Anna graduated from the A. N. Kosygin Moscow State Textile University, she then continued her studies at the University of Fashion in Lyon, France and the Academy of Design in Lodz, Poland. In 2010, she founded her own label, whose success has led her to show collections in the Russian Fashion Week and the Volvo-Moscow Fashion Week.

ANTONIO ALVARADO
www.antonioalvarado.es

Antonio Alvarado from Alicante, Spain moved to Madrid in the eighties, where he revolutionized the way of presenting collections in clubs and designed costumes for movies such as those of Pedro Almodóvar. He has been a fixture at the Cibeles Madrid Fashion Week since 1984 and his collections, characterized by a meticulous pattern design and attention to detail, have appeared in the pages of the likes of *Vanity Fair*. For five years, he was the president of ModaFAD, a launching pad for young fashion designers.

ASGER JUEL LARSEN
www.asgerjuellarsen.com

Since graduating with a BA in menswear from London College of Fashion, the Danish designer Asger Juel Larsen has enjoyed a lot of media attention as well as being listed amongst the finalists at the prestigious Mittelmoda awards. His collections explore expressions of masculine strength marked by hard contrasts, such as stiff structures with delicate fabrics. This dichotomy is also reflected through futuristic materials such as leather, PVC, rubber cords, and different types of metal.

ASHER LEVINE
www.asherlevine.com

Born in Florida, U.S., Asher developed a fascination with fashion from an early age. In 2006, he moved to New York, where he studied managerial entrepreneurship at Pace University. During the same time Asher began to independently create conceptual designs that could be seen on different personalities across the New York underground club circuit. With several menswear collections on the market, Asher defies fashion industry standards and the physical limitations of the garments.

BEBA'S CLOSET
www. bebascloset.com

In 2002, the Spanish designer Belén Barbero decided to renounce her career as an economist and devote her time entirely to fashion. She studied at the Istituto Europeo di Design in Madrid, Spain and in her last year she won the prize for best collection awarded by Burberry. After working for several labels, she opened her own atelier in Madrid in 2006 and since 2010 she has taken part in runways such as El Ego de Cibeles Madrid Fashion Week, with very fresh and feminine concepts. Currently she is working with the designer Miguel Palacio.

BERNARD CHANDRAN
www.bernardchandran.com

At age sixteen he began studying Fashion Design in Petaling Jaya, Malaysia. After perfecting his technique in Paris, France he returned home to open a small store in 1993, now a couture house with very loyal followers. Awards such as the Look of the Year from the Open European Contest or Designer of the Year at the Malaysian International Fashion Awards support his successful career. He is also a major television personality as he has taken the part of mentor in the reality show *Project Runway Malaysia*.

BIBIAN BLUE
www.bibianblue.com

Bibian Blue, a native of Barcelona, Spain, trained as a graphic designer in the Escola Massana in her hometown, and completed a number of courses at the Academia Internacional de la Moda and later postgraduate work at FD Moda. She is an icon of vintage, retro and burlesque aesthetics, and the corset is her fetish garment. In 2000, she launched her successful first collection and now has points of sale throughout Europe, worldwide online distribution, and a boutique-atelier in the center of Barcelona.

BOHENTO
www.bohento.com

Cuca Ferrá studied Fashion Design, specializing in leather, at the Centro Superior de Diseño de Moda in Madrid, Spain. Later, she worked for several fashion labels and furthered her studies in plastic arts. In 2008, together with her former partner Pablo de la Torre, she created Bohento. They present their very individual collections at the El Ego de Cibeles Madrid Fashion Week. Currently, Cuca is going solo at the forefront of Bohento while working as a fashion design professor at the Polytechnic University of Madrid.

BORA AKSU
www.boraaksu.com

London-based Turkish designer Bora Aksu graduated from Central Saint Martins. His graduation runway show won the sponsorship that prompted him to create his own brand, whose debut was the fall/winter 2003 collection during London Fashion Week. *The Guardian* rated his runway presentation as "one of the top five shows in London." Since then, he has received the New Generation Award four times from the British Fashion Council.

CAMILLA NORRBACK
www.camillanorrback.com

At the age of thirteen Camilla Norrback, born in Finland and now settled in Switzerland, got her first sewing machine and since then she knew that she wanted to dedicate her life to fashion. Camilla Norrback is a well-known label in Switzerland and has been nominated for major fashion awards. Since 2002, Camilla has been committed to creating ecologically sustainable garments called Ecoluxury. In addition to the female collection that she presents at the Stockholm Fashion Week, she created a male line, Norrback, in 2010.

CARLOS DÍEZ
www.myspace.com/diezdiez

Carlos Díez Díez was born in Bilbao, Spain, but moved to Madrid, where he now has his studio-atelier. His style is totally creative and original. He has worked for designer Antonio Alvarado and since 2006 he has created a sportswear collection each season for the American label Converse. In 2004, he began to show-case his collections at the Cibeles Madrid Fashion Week, where he won the L'Oréal award for the best collection in 2006. In 2009 he opened his first store in the Spanish capital.

CATI SERRÀ
www.catiserra.com

Cati Serrà was born in Majorca, Spain. She is a graduate from the ESDi School of Design in Barcelona, Spain receiving the Gold Medal for the best student in her class. She interned with Miguel Adrover and in 2008, she worked alongside him for the presentation of his collection at New York Fashion Week. That same year she founded her menswear and womenswear label, known for its comfort, elegance, and careful design. She shows her collections at El Ego de Cibeles Madrid Fashion Week.

CHARLIE LE MINDU
www.charlielemindu.com

Charlie Le Mindu was born in France. He was a hair-dressing prodigy during his time at the French Hair Academy until he became a fashion stylist in Berlin, a true master of *haute-coiffure*. In 2009, he wowed with his first fashion collection at London Fashion Week, with an immediate response from magazines around the world, such as *Vogue Italia*, *Vogue Hommes Japan*, and *i-D*. He currently is the star of a successful show on KonbiniTV, *Charlie's Treatment*.

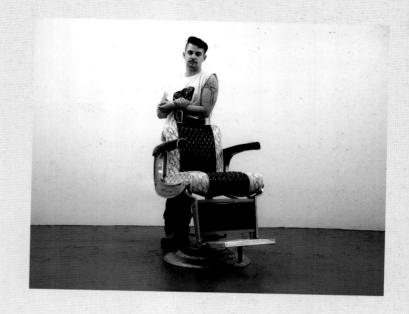

CRAIG LAURENCE
www.craiglawrence.co.uk

Craig Lawrence is a knitwear designer, born in Ipswich, United Kingdom, and based in London. He graduated from Central Saint Martins. Over six seasons, he produced knitwear for Gareth Pugh, before establishing his own label. With his debut at London Fashion Week, Craig was awarded the New Generation sponsorship by the British Fashion Council, a support he has had for four seasons. He has recently participated in London Show Rooms, an initiative that encourages the presence of young London designers in New York.

DAWID TOMASZEWSKI
www.dawid-tomaszewski.com

Dawid was born in Poland. He studied at the London College of Fashion and the Akademie der Künste in Berlin, having studied art history at Poznan. During his studies, he worked for Sonia Rykiel and when he finished, he worked for companies such as Reebok, in Boston, and Comme des Garçons, in Paris, until he founded his own label in 2009. His first collection won the Young Designer Award at Berlin Fashion Week. Tomaszewki's proposals have been influenced by art, architecture, and a passion for jazz.

DESIGNSKOLEN KOLDING
www.designskolenkolding.dk

Danish design represents a mark of quality and a reputation that goes far beyond the borders of its country. The work of Designskolen Kolding helps to strengthen the position of Danish fashion design, both nationally and internationally, by training young designers at the forefront of Danish fashion and by creating interesting concepts and proposals. His collections, presented at the Copenhagen Fashion Week, stand out for their studied pattern design, impossible shapes, and surprising details. The following designers are featured in this book:

Beate Godager
Anne Mette Kjærgaard Jensen
Mette Daring fashion & Mette Gliemann textile
Mette Marie Krarup Bertelsen
Linda Gunnarsson
Sidse Bordal
Siff Pristed Nielsen
Sophie Lassen
Lisbeth Grosen Nielsen
Alexandra Lindek
Betina Møller
Anja Merete Larsen

DIANA DORADO
www.dianadorado.com

The Colombian designer Diana Dorado is based in Barcelona, Spain where she studied fashion design at the ESDi School of Design. She has won the Moda-FAD award for best designer and has participated in the 080 Barcelona Fashion, the Pasarela Abierta de Murcia, and El Ego de Cibeles Madrid Fashion Week. Diana Dorado has earned herself a place among the great revelations of Spanish fashion with colorful, urban, and very feminine designs.

DIMITRI BY DIMITRIOS PANAGIOTOPOULOS
www.bydimitri.com

The Greek-Italian designer Dimitri Panagiotopoulos from the South Tyrol studied at the famous fashion school ESMOD and later earned a master's degree in fashion design at the Istituto Marangoni in Milan, Italy. After working for prestigious labels like Jil Sander, Hugo Boss, and Vivienne Westwood, he opened his first store in the center of Merano, Italy, and currently presents two annual collections of harmonic and feminine garments at the Mercedes-Benz Fashion Week Berlin.

EK THONGPRASERT
www.ekthongprasert.be

Ek Thongprasert was born in Bangkok, Thailand. After completing his first degree in architecture, he attended one of the most famous fashion schools, the Royal Academy of Fine Arts in Antwerp, Belgium, which has produced many famous designers. In 2008, he created his eponymous label with a strong conceptual approach, along with jewelry designer Noon Passama, whom he met during his first degree at the University of Chulalongkorn, one of the most prestigious in Thailand.

ELENA PRZHONSKAYA
www.przhonskaya.com

Elena Przhonskaya was born in Ukraine. She graduated from the Kyiv National University of Technology and Design in 2007. During her studies, she won several competitions for young designers in Ukraine and Russia and participated in the nationally televised project *PRO-fashion*. After graduating, she opened her own studio in the center of Kiev with the aim of developing a strong brand with an international vision. Since then Elena has been a regular at the Ukrainian Fashion Week.

ELENA SKANKUN
naum_ann@bk.ru

The Russian designer Elena Skankun boasts an excellent track record. She won the Russian Silhouette in 2003 and has presented collections on international runways such as Roma Altamoda, thanks to an internship in the Saga Design Center of Saga Furs. She is also the director of the Khanty-Mansiysk International Fashion institution. Her collections, present at the Moscow Fashion Week, stand out for their elegance and mastery of her favorite materials, tulle and leather.

ELISA PALOMINO
www.elisapalomino.com

This Valencian studied at Central Saint Martins in London. After several years working at Moschino, she moved to Paris. For eight years she was director of the John Galliano studio, while also working at the Christian Dior Haute Couture collection. In 2008, after collaborating with Roberto Cavalli, she moved to New York to become vice president of design for Diane von Furstenberg. In 2010, she created her own label and showed her collections in New York and Cibeles Madrid Fashion Weeks.

ERICA ZAIONTS
www.ericazaionts.com

A Ukrainian designer based in Moscow, Erica Zaionts graduated from the A. N. Kosygin Moscow State Textile University. Her label is a family business founded in 2001 and among its main virtues are its self-made manufacturing. Erica is considered as one of the few Russian designers who creates top quality prêt-à-porter clothing. Her collections, shown at Moscow Fashion Week, are characterized by their powerful image and recognizable style that is based on the practicality of forms.

EWA I WALLA
www.ewaiwalla.se

The Swedish womenswear label Ewa i Walla was established in the early nineties. The designer Ewa Iwalla creates unique garments inspired by the romanticism of the seventeenth century, haute couture, and rural culture, and always seeks to achieve an unexpected result. Her collections, distinguished by natural fabrics like cotton, linen, silk, and wool, are showcased at Stockholm Fashion Week and are present in eighteen countries through some 320 establishments, including two of her own stores in Stockholm.

G.V.G.V.
www.gvgv.jp

Mug, the Japanese designer behind G.V.G.V., graduated from the Kuwasawa Design School. The label, founded in 1999, stands out for its mix of masculinity and femininity, and conveys great sensitivity each season. G.V.G.V. is one of the most sought after fashion labels in Tokyo and is a regular during Japan Fashion Week. In addition, Mug is a regular contributor injecting her creativity into other fashion houses.

GEORGIA HARDINGE
www.georgiahardinge.co.uk

Born in London, the daughter of Lord Nick Hardinge and Baroness Florence von Oppenheim grew up traveling and developing her fascination with fashion. She studied at Parsons School in Paris and won the Golden Thimble for her graduation collection. After her return to London, she founded her label in 2009. The launch of her debut collection took place in the independent ON|OFF runway during London Fashion Week. With the experience of several collections behind her, Georgia has achieved an elegant style marked by architectural touches.

HARRYHALIM
www.hhharryhalim.com

Born in Indonesia and now based in Paris, his first collection won the Asian Young Fashion Designers Contest and he was a finalist in the Mercedes-Benz Asia Fashion Awards in 2005. Later he designed for a commercial fashion house while working on his own collections and perfecting his meticulous technique. In 2008, Harry Halim was awarded Best Young Asian Designer of the Year, which catapulted him to Paris where he currently shows his modern and romantic collections with a halo of dark sensuality.

HASAN HEJAZI
www.hasanhejazi.co.uk

Hasan Hejazi was born in Manchester, England. He studied Fine Arts for three years and then decided to move into Fashion Design at Manchester Metropolitan University. He completed a masters in fashion design from London College of Fashion. His graduation collection was a success: he was a finalist in Manchester Awards for the best designer fashion and showcased his collection at Harrods Launches. His second collection has an army of celebrity followers, including Kylie Minogue.

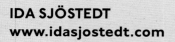

IDA SJÖSTEDT
www.idasjostedt.com

Ida Sjöstedt was born in Stockholm, Sweden. She moved to London and graduated in fashion design at Westminster University. In 2001, Ida returned to Sweden and in August of that year she launched her first collection during Stockholm Fashion Week. She has become a regular on this runway since then and also exhibits in Paris during the prêt-à-porter fashion weeks. The combination of tasteful kitsch and elegance describe Ida's design philosophy. Her aim is to create beautiful clothes for women who want fashion to be fun.

ION FIZ
www.ionfiz.com

Ion Fiz was born in Bilbao, Spain. He studied at the International School of Fashion Design and Moda Lanca in his native city and has worked for companies such as Karhu, Bonaventure, Elisa Amann, and the renowned Pertegaz. After launching his own label, his career has been unstoppable, and has won awards such as the FAD Award for Best Designer, the Prix de la Moda Marie Claire and the L'Oréal Paris Cibeles prize. His proposals have a unique and sophisticated hallmark, which he shows season after season at the Cibeles Madrid Fashion Week.

J JS LEE
www.jsleelondon.com

Jackie JS Lee, born in Seoul, Korea, moved to London to study a postgraduate degree in pattern design at Central Saint Martins. After two years as a pattern designer for Kisa London, she returned to the same school to complete a master's degree. Her graduate collection received rave reviews from the press and buyers, and she was awarded the revered Harrods Award. Later she launched her label J JS Lee, featuring sleek and chic androgynous pieces designed for modern, feminine women.

JEAN//PHILLIP
www.jeanphillip.dk

Jean//phillip is a fashion label based in Copenhagen and founded by Jean-Phillip in 2007. The main objective of the label is menswear, but each collection also includes a few outfits for women. The Jean//phillip label is both modern and minimalist with a slim cut to create a sense of subtle androgyny suitable for both men and women. Classic tailoring, haute couture, and attention to detail are the hallmarks of the designer and his work.

JUANJO OLIVA
www.juanjooliva.com

Juanjo Oliva was born in Madrid. He graduated with a degree in fashion design from the Institución Artística de Enseñanza and took a course in fashion illustration at Parsons School of Design in New York. During the nineties he worked for companies such as Isabel Berz, Zara, Helena Rohner, Antonio Pernas, Sybilla, and Amaya Arzuaga. In 2000, he opened his store in Madrid and since 2003 he has showcased his collections at Cibeles Madrid Fashion Week. He has received awards such as the Best L'Oréal Collection, which he has been awarded twice, and the T de Telva for the Best National Designer.

JULIUS
www.julius-garden.jp

The Japanese designer Tastsuro Horikawa started his own line in 1996, creating his first fashion company, Nuke. In 2001, Julius was born as an art project that eventually became a large fashion project combined with video art. Its first appearance was in 2004 in Tokyo Collection. It has become a cult label on account of its gothic style, with black as its trademark color, exploring the spiritual and modern side of the designer.

KARLOTA LASPALAS
www.karlotalaspalas.com

Karlota Laspalas was born in Pamplona, Spain. Since graduating from the Felicidad Duce School of Fashion and Design, her career has known no limits. She has presented her collections on runways such as 080 Barcelona Fashion, where she received the award for best menswear collection, El Ego de Cibeles Madrid Fashion Week, Creamoda in Bilbao, Createurope in Berlin, and Mittelmoda in Gorizia, Italy. Her designs, with a bohemian-urban style, have won over both the public and press wherever she exhibits.

KRIS VAN ASSCHE
www.krisvanassche.com

Born in Belgium, Kris Van Assche is a graduate of the Royal Academy of Fine Arts in Antwerp, Belgium and later joined Hedi Slimane's team at YSL in Paris. When Slimane joined Dior Homme in 2003, Van Assche followed suit. In 2005, he created his own label and in 2007 he was appointed artistic director of Dior Homme, combining both jobs perfectly. Kris Van Assche has a unique approach to sportswear, blending luxurious and functional materials for a modern and sophisticated man.

LEMONIEZ
www.lemoniez.com

Fernando Lemoniez was born in San Sebastian, Spain where, in 1985, he opened a boutique-atelier with his own collections. He later moved to Paris, and attended a training course at Yves Saint Laurent Haute Couture and presented his collections within the official calendar of the Chambre Syndicale de la Couture. Between 1991 and 1998, he joined forces with Miguel Palacio to create Palacio & Lemoniez, a label that used to showcase its collections at Cibeles Madrid, where he has presented his solo runway shows since 1999.

MAISON MARTIN MARGIELA
www.maisonmartinmargiela.com

The label was founded in 1988 by Martin Margiela, a graduate from the Royal Academy of Fine Arts in Antwerp, Belgium and creative director of Hermès, and Jenny Meirens, assistant to Jean Paul Gaultier. A must-have collection at Paris Fashion Week, and having celebrated its twentieth anniversary, Maison Martin Margiela continues to wow with unique propositions and international repercussions. With Renzo Rosso now at the forefront of the label, a new era of creative identity can be expected without overlooking the essence of the mythical house.

MAL-AIMÉE
www.mal-aimee.com

Léonie Hostettler and Marius Borgeaud met in ateliers of the Geneva University of Art and Design. They have been working together since their beginnings at Nina Ricci with Olivier Theyskens. In 2010, they presented their first womenswear collection in Paris under the name of Mal-Aimée. They experiment with volumes and lines, paying particular attention to the choice of colors and fabrics. Simultaneously poetic, romantic, sporty, and urban, their proposals oscillate between extreme femininity and elegant androgyny.

MALAFACHA BRAND
malafacha.blogspot.com

The Mexican designers Francisco Saldaña and Víctor Hernal are the duo behind Malafacha Brand, a male and female clothing label. Francisco studied fashion design and Victor studied visual communication, and both disciplines have helped in developing a product with a very personal style. Winners of the prize for best womenswear collection in the Mexico Fashion Awards for their fall/winter 2008/2009 collection, they present their collections at Mercedes-Benz Fashion Week Mexico.

MALINI RAMANI
www.maliniramani.com

Born in New York, Malini Ramani spent a few years in India and then returned to her hometown to study fashion buying and merchandising at the Fashion Institute of Technology. She then decided to create her own label in India. Her philosophy is to design clothes that she would wear herself. She believes in glamorous, vibrant colors and plunging necklines. She has her own stores in India and Bali, and her collections are sold in cities around the world, including Hong Kong, Monte Carlo, and New York.

MANISH ARORA
www.manisharora.ws

Manish Arora is considered the John Galliano of India. He studied at the National Institute of Fashion Technology and founded his firm in 1997. In 2002, he opened his first store in New Delhi and the following year another one in Bombay. His success and international prestige and his regular presence in the fashion weeks in India and London led him to open new stores and to sell in more than eighty stores worldwide. His blend of Indian tradition with western silhouettes and eccentric colors are the trademarks of the label.

MARCEL OSTERTAG
www.marcelostertag.com

Marcel Ostertag was born in Berchtesgaden, Germany. After completing his studies in ESMOD Munich, he graduated from Central Saint Martins. He then decided to create his own label, whose spectacular debut in 2006 was praised by the press and recognized with awards such as Moët & Chandon Fashion Debut and the Karstadt New Generation Award. Today, he has his own store in Munich and his collections are presented during the official calendar of the Mercedes-Benz Fashion Week Berlin.

MARK FAST
www.markfast.net

The Canadian knitwear designer Mark Fast studied for five years at Central Saint Martins in London. He has created knitwear for Bora Aksu, a collaboration that spanned three seasons, and has worked with Stuart Vevers for the Loewe fall/winter 2009 show and with Christian Louboutin on shoes for his spring/summer 2010 collection. His collections, which combine different techniques and innovative materials, are exhibited at London Fashion Week and featured in magazines such as *Vogue*, *i-D* and *Another Magazine*.

MARTA MONTOTO
www.martamontoto.com

The young Spanish designer Marta Montoto, born in Galicia, comes from a family background in textile. Her family has worked in knitwear since the fifties, so she dares to experiment and redefine concepts using this technique that she dominates so well. She studied fashion design at ESDEGMA. After completing work experience in Armand Basi, she has decided to design highly creative collections for men, with naïve touches, which have earned her a place on runways such as El Ego de Cibeles Madrid Fashion Week.

MARTIN LAMOTHE
www.martinlamothe.es

Elena Martin was born in Barcelona, Span. She graduated from the Escola d'Arts i Tècniques de la Moda in her native city, and later studied art history and earned an honors degree at the Southampton Art School. She then moved to London and studied at Central Saint Martins. After graduation, Elena worked with Alexander McQueen, Vivienne Westwood, and Robert Cary-Williams. In 2006, she launched her label Martin Lamothe, with an impeccable career and appearances on runways in Berlin, Barcelona, Paris, and Madrid.

MAYA HANSEN
www.mayahansen.com

Maya Hansen was born in Madrid, Spain. She graduated with honors at the CSDMM in Madrid in 2002, after having already received some recognition. After experience in Javier Larraínzar's atelier, she founded her label in 2004 and since 2006, she has specialized in corsetry. She has presented her proposals in fairs, such as Erotica UK, that bring together the world's best corset makers and has earned her a spot in the Cibeles Madrid Fashion Week calendar.

NEREA LURGAIN
www.nerealurgain.com

Nerea Lurgain was born in San Sebastian, Spain. She graduated in fine arts in Lejona and fashion design in IDEP Barcelona. Nerea works in different areas of design and art, which give her ideas, sources of inspiration, and design mechanisms that differentiate her with a unique and personal way to project items. She has presented collections at 080 Barcelona Fashion Week, the Dalian International Show in China, the Cibeles Madrid Fashion Week, and the China International Garment & Textile Fair.

OMAR KASHOURA
www.omarkashoura.com

Born in Leeds, United Kingdom of Arab descent, Omar Kashoura graduated with honors from the London College of Fashion with a collection that won him the award for best menswear designer in New York's Gen Art Style. He worked for labels such as Preen and Unconditional, and in 2006 he completed his masters at Central Saint Martins. Since the launch of his successful label, he has received awards such as the Deutsche Bank Pyramid Award and the NewGen from the British Fashion Council for two consecutive seasons.

QASIMI
www.qasimi.com

From the United Arab Emirates, Khalid Al Qasimi grew up influenced by the sophistication of the Middle East. In 2001, he graduated in Hispanic studies and French literature at University College London, and later decided to study fashion design at Central Saint Martins. Since 2008, he has presented several womenswear and menswear collections in the London Fashion Week, and since 2009 he has been on the calendar of the Paris Men's Fashion Week. Currently he concentrates on men's fashion.

RICARDO DOURADO
www.ricardodourado.com

Ricardo Dourado was born in Portugal. He completed his studies in 2003 at CITEX Oporto. He has worked in studios such as Osvaldo Martins, Lidija Kolovrat, and Helena de Matos. In 2004, Ricardo established his own atelier, and has since presented his collections at ModaLisboa Fashion Week. He is also a member of the design team Polopique, a fashion company based in Portugal, Brazil, and Spain. His work conveys a casual elegance and challenges conventional forms

SINPATRON
www.sinpatron.com

As the name suggests, the Spanish company, created by Alberto Etxebarrieta from Bilbao, is characterized by modeling his garments, because it gives him greater freedom than patternmaking does. He studied tourism in his hometown and dramatic art in Edinburgh, until his life "without patterns" led him to fashion. He is self-taught and a craftsman. He created the label Sinpatron in 2004 and presents his collections at the Cibeles Madrid Fashion Week with bold, colorful and unisex concepts.

SPIJKERS EN SPIJKERS
www.spijkersenspijkers.nl

The Dutch twin sisters Truus and Riet created the label Spijkers en Spijkers in 2000, after graduating from the School of Arts in Arnhem. For their debut collection, they were awarded the Robijn Fashion Award, and they completed a master's at the Fashion Institute in the same city. Inspired by their idols, Schiaparelli and Vionnet, they use their individuality with a common vision, thus achieving solid, clear, and geometric forms highlighting the female figure. They have presented their collections in London, Amsterdam, and Milan.

STAS LOPATKIN
www.lopatkin.ru

Stas Lopatkin was born in Leningrad, Russia. He studied at the School of Sewing and Graphic Arts Department of the Herzen State Pedagogical University of Russia. After graduating, he began with theatrical costume design and private orders, until he created his own label in 2001. He made his debut in 2003 at the Saint Petersburg Fashion Week, and has since showcased his collections for the Russian and European public with proposals that always combine elegance and fine art as a hallmark.

THE SWEDISH SCHOOL OF TEXTILES
www.hb.se

In the Swedish School of Textiles of the University of Borås, fashion design is understood in its broadest sense. The school provides a unique environment for reaching maturity as a designer and artist. This book features the collections created by designers who passed through its classrooms in recent years and who presented their collections in the spring/summer 2011 edition of Stockholm Fashion Week. The proposals and concepts are a sign of creativity and the immense talent of these young designers.

Sara Andersson - Prepositions
Johanna Milvert - View
Elin Klevmar - Efterklang
Stina Randestad - Breed
Emelie Johansson - Structure is everything
Jennie Siljedahl - Control me as I control you
Elin Sundling - I paint myself into a corner
Ellinor Nilsen - Nobodies
Charlotta Mattsson - Welcome to Uchronia
David Söderlund - Homage
Helena Quist - Ubuntu

HÖGSKOLAN I BORÅS
VETENSKAP FÖR PROFESSION

TIM VAN STEENBERGEN
www.timvansteenbergen.com

The Belgian designer Tim Van Steenbergen graduated from the Royal Academy of Fine Arts in Antwerp. Afterwards he studied draping and haute couture and worked as chief assistant for Olivier Theyskens. In 2002, he presented his first collection in Paris and created his own label. In addition to his magnificent collections, Tim creates costumes for major movie and theater productions worldwide. In 2009 he was voted best Belgian designer in the Elle Style Awards.

TSUMORI CHISATO
www.tsumorichisato.com

Born in Japan, Tsumori Chisato studied at the prestigious Bunka Fashion College in Tokyo. She worked as head designer for the Issey Miyake Sports line, later renamed I. S. Chisato Tsumori Design. In 1990, she presented her own collection, Tsumori Chisato, at Japan Fashion Week, where it was a total success. In 2003, she presented her menswear collection and became part of the official calendar of the Paris Fashion Week with innovation, elegance, and fun as hallmarks.

VASSILIOS KOSTETSOS
www.kostetsos.gr

Vassilios Kostetsos was born in Athens, Greece where his mother had a leading fashion import business. By the age of nine, he visited the studio and was enchanted with this magical world. In 1990, he created his own label and presented his first haute couture collection with excellent results. He has presented runway shows in places as special as the Central Railway Station of Athens, and his collections have received critical claim from followers in New York.

VICTORIO & LUCCHINO
www.victorioylucchino.com

José Luis Medina del Corral, from Seville, Spain and José Víctor Rodríguez, from Córdoba, Spain, created Victorio & Lucchino in the late seventies. There are six elements that define their unmistakable style: color, lace, embellishment defined by fringing, flounce, brides with their own identity, and the fusion of tradition from Southern Spain with cutting-edge fashion. Their proposals are shown each season at the Cibeles Madrid Fashion Week and have been presented on the runways of New York, Milan, Barcelona, Germany, and Japan, among others.

VLADISLAV AKSENOV
www.vladislavaksenov.com

The Russian designer Vladislav Aksenov created his menswear company in 2007. He broke conceptions with his first collection, zero zero one, in Saint Petersburg Fashion Week, with a style that blends luxury and military style. The label has two lines: the first, Vladislav Aksenov, for serious and respectable people; the second line, Varan, is for those who prefer an unusual and daring temperament. In addition, Vladislav also devotes part of his creative energy to interior design.

VRL COLLECTION
www.vrl-collection.jimdo.com

Born in Cadiz, Spain, Paco Varela is the fashion designer and stylist behind the firm VRL Collection, based in Madrid. After his experience working for the Portuguese designer Alexandra, he set up his own company. His collections have been presented in various editions of Pasarela Costello in Madrid, Jovens Criadores in Lisbon, and South 36-32N in Cadiz. He focuses on romantic and elegant collections for men and women with a predominance of light and transparent fabrics.